Sandra Lee
semi-homemade®

cooking

Meredith® Books Des Moines, Iowa

Library of Congress Control Number 2005921341 ISBN: 0-696-22685-5 Published by Meredith® Books. Des Moines, Iowa.

dedication

This book is dedicated to my grandma,
Lorraine Korth Waldroop,
whose love, guidance, and example made me the person I am.
How fortunate I was to have you.
S.L.

special thanks

Peggy and Bill Singlehurst, my aunt and uncle, for all your love and support

Kimber Lee, my sister, who's always been there for me or gone there for me, I love you

Cynthia Christi-Lee, my sister, for sharing your most precious creations so unselfishly

Rich and John Paul Christiansen, my brothers, I'm so proud of you both

Lee Gaskill and Michele Christiansen, for being such wonderful additions to our family

Scottie, Danielle, Brandon, Austen, Stephanie, Taner, Brycer, Blakey, and Katie,
my nieces and nephews, who are sweeter than any dessert I could ever make

Colleen Schmidt, my best friend, for all the chili dogs, corn dogs, root beer floats, dreams, & confidences

Zane Rothschild, my mentor, whose little nudges along the way help me choose the right paths

Aspen, my baby dog, who owns my heart and is as cute as a cupcake

acknowledgement

Photographers: Ed Ouellette, George Lange, Maryellen Baker, and Joe Buissink;
Layout and Design: Hilary Lentini

Stylists: Jeff Parker, Norman Stewart, DoHan Rogers, Wes Martin, Laurent Saint Cricq, Jules Kaye,
Angie Ketterman, Robin Tucker, Lisa Barnet, and Maryann Lesser

Production Team: Jan Miller, Mick Schnepf, Pamela Acuff, Amy Nichols, Erin Burns, Jessica Saari,
Matt Strelecki, Jim Blume, Jeff Meyers, Lisa Shotland, Doug Guendel, Bob Mate, and Jack Griffin

Table of Contents

Chapter 1

Breakfast
16

Chapter 2

Lunch
38

Chapter 3

Dinner
58

Chapter 4

Appetizers & Cocktails
76

Chapter 5

Soups and Salads
110

Introduction from Wolfgang Puck

As a chef, one of the comments I hear most often from my customers is that they don't have enough time to cook at home anymore. That's why I'm so happy to see that my friend Sandra Lee has come up with her own unique solution to that problem.

Sandra starts with a wide assortment of convenience foods that you can find in any supermarket—preshredded carrots, bottled lemon juice, frozen puff pastry, fresh pastas, pregrated cheeses, canned soups and sauces, boxed cake and pudding mixes, and more. She puts these everyday ingredients together, adds a generous measure of her own talent, creativity, and flair, and the results are astonishing. Not only do her recipes look good, but they taste delicious too.

While I have many sous chefs in my restaurants, chopping, dicing, making stocks, mixing doughs, and so on, Sandra puts the entire American food industry to work for you. So, no matter how busy you are, in Sandra's book you will always find delicious-tasting shortcuts. Her "Semi-Homemade" approach will help bring you, your family, and friends back into the kitchen and to the dinner table, no matter how busy you may be.

Sandra's approach to cooking is filled with a sense of fun and a love of sharing good food with others. Her enthusiasm is contagious, and her warm personality shines from every page of this book.

Live, love, eat … and have the time to enjoy it all!

Wolfgang Puck

Letter from Sandra

Semi-Homemade Cooking is all about you. A philosophy that will make your life much easier than it's ever been before! I've spent the past fifteen years creating a Semi-Homemade lifestyle for myself—and now for you—busy people on the go and on a budget. Our days are filled with too much to do, too little time to do it in, and not enough money to make it all happen. Life today requires us all to be super-human. "To-do" lists have gone from one-page handwritten sheets to entire chapters in a hardbound book. And after getting all your "to-dos" done, you're expected to plan, shop for, and whip up new, fresh, mouth-watering homemade meals from scratch?

What is Semi-Homemade cooking? It's a new way of cooking where nothing is made from scratch. The Semi-Homemade cooking approach is easily done by combining several prepackaged foods, a few fresh ingredients, and a "pinch of this with a hint of that" to make new, easy, gourmet-tasting, inexpensive meals in minutes. It's fast, fabulous food.

How will Semi-Homemade Cooking make your life easier? Each recipe comes complete with time estimates for planning along with a suggested brand-name list of ingredients to ease your shopping load. So whether you are cooking for two or twenty, there will always be something easy, quick, and affordable to prepare. You'll be the "Julia Child" of your own kitchen without the time, energy, and expense it normally requires.

What will you get here that you can't get anywhere else? You'll get an entirely new way of cooking. You'll get recipes complete with actual brand names of products to use so you can be sure the recipes you create taste exactly like they should, every time. You'll get the benefit of quality and taste without the stress traditional cooking creates.

I'd love to hear your thoughts, ideas, questions, or suggestions. I've included my address and e-mail for your convenience (see page 240). Welcome to the new Semi-Homemade world—I hope you will enjoy all the extra time you'll have!

With a warm hug,

Sandra Lee

Smart Shopping

Grocery shopping can be made so much easier by including the following helpful hints and timesaving tricks into your routine:

Plan your entire week's menu in advance. This takes a bit of effort, but is sure to help you avoid stress later.

Try to do all your shopping on one day and stay away from shopping at peak hours. (Remember to clip those Sunday coupons—they'll save you a bundle.)

It's best to load your cart with nonperishables first, followed by produce, dairy products, meats and seafood, then finish up with frozen foods on top. Getting in and out of the grocery store can be much quicker if you create a shopping list and organize it by categories such as packaged goods, baked goods, canned and jarred products, produce, meats, dairy, frozen foods, household products, and cleaning items. Creating this aisle-by-aisle shopping guide will surely make you more efficient.

Check the dates of all perishable items. Purchase containers that have the longest indicated dates of expiration.

Purchase produce that is just ripe, or almost ripe, based on when they will be served (advance weekly menus come in handy here). Be careful when purchasing fully ripe or overripe produce, it can go bad instantly.

Saving money can be simpler than you think. By clipping just a couple of coupons and signing up for free membership discount cards, given at most larger grocery store chains, you're sure to save a surprising sum.

Get your groceries home and into the refrigerator or freezer quickly. If you plan on doing other errands before going home, bring along a thermal cooler to keep chilled foods cool. (Bag all frozen and refrigerator items together to keep them cool longer.)

Try not to shop on an empty stomach. When hungry, you're more likely to make impulse purchases, spending more money and time than you anticipated. If you're famished, visit the deli or bakery department for a smart snack before shopping.

Disposables

Making life easier can be so simple if you utilize disposable products. Paper plates, napkins, plastic utensils, baking dishes, serving bowls and platters are all readily available. Disposable items provide quick preparation and cleanup—you'll minimize your work while maximizing your leisure time.

Brand Names

Stylish, quality cooking is made easy when using our suggestions for preselected and tested name-brand foods. These precombined ingredient sources reduce expenses and enhance taste. Substitutions, of course, are always at your discretion. Brand-name suggestions are highlighted in italics throughout each recipe and are available through most major grocery store chains.

Prepping, Cooking & Cooling Times

Time is on your side. Each quick, easy recipe comes complete with time estimates for prepping, cooking, and cooling. You decide how much time you want to spend in your kitchen: a new luxury you're sure to utilize, appreciate, and enjoy.

Safe Slow Cooking

Follow these basic guidelines for no-fail slow cooking:

• Cooking time depends on the setting you choose. The recipes that cook for 4 hours on high will take 7 to 8 hours on low. If you want food to cook all day, select the low setting.

• A slow cooker needs liquid to cook. Add juice, broth, wine or spirits instead of water to enhance flavor. Because wine and liquors evaporate during cooking leaving only flavor, these dishes are family-friendly.

• To avoid cracking the pot, put cold ingredients into a cold slow cooker and warm ingredients into a preheated slow cooker. Always follow manufacturer's instructions for best results.

Leftovers

Food can be even more delicious the second time around. When stored properly and reheated slowly, food frequently tends to taste better with time. Reheatable leftovers should be placed in shallow storage containers, which allow food to cool. Transfer to glass or ceramic containers if reheating in the microwave oven. Recipes that make great leftovers are noted with instructions for serving a second time.

Storage

Reusable plastic storage containers are convenient, airtight, and lock in freshness and guarantee food lasts longer. They are perfect to use in the pantry and refrigerator. For freezer storage, be sure to use plastic storage containers that are labeled specifically for the freezer. Label all containers with contents and date. Store do-ahead dinners and leftovers in shallow containers. See the simple storage suggestions that accompany many recipes.

Wines

A good wine, whether expensive or not, warms the way to ending the day. It's a palate-pleaser before, during, or after dinner and a relaxing way to enjoy a weekend lunch or an afternoon brunch. Try the suggested wines and soon you, too, will feel as knowledgeable as any connoisseur.

Serving & Cooking

Dijon Chicken and Mushrooms
page 60 De Loach® Chardonnay

Steak Pinwheels with Sun-Dried Tomato Stuffing and Rosemary Mashed Potatoes page 63
Kendall-Jackson® Cabernet Sauvignon

Lemon Turkey Cutlets page 65
Chateau St. Michelle® Chardonnay

Sweet-and-Sour Pork Kabobs with Fried Rice page 66 Hugel® Gentil

Mushroom Steak and Sweet Mash
page 69 Columbia Crest® Cabernet Sauvignon

Tropical Salmon page 70
Meridian® Chardonnay

Speedy Swedish Meatballs
page 72 Sonoma Creek® Merlot

Noodles Alfredo page 75
Beringer North Coast® Zinfandel

Breakfast

Breakfast, as they say, is the most important meal of the day. This may be true, but try to convince yourself to sit down for five minutes and eat when you're running late and can't even see straight. Growing up, I was fine with Cap'n Crunch® and milk—that much sugar will give anyone plenty of energy … for awhile. But the nutritional value, or lack thereof, will send your energy crashing way before lunchtime. Still, I must admit, a sugar-filled breakfast of Cap'n Crunch® is better than no breakfast at all.

Without breakfast, you feel exhausted even after a great night's sleep. You find yourself becoming easily irritable and having difficulty concentrating. A bad morning, or even a bad day, cannot always be blamed on waking up on the wrong side of the bed. Rather, it may be contributed to trying to function properly and at full capacity without giving your body what it needs: fuel.

This chapter is filled with delicious, simple breakfast choices that will jump-start your day. Some are sugar-filled (because I couldn't resist), and most can be prepared the night before and reheated the next day to make your precious morning moments even more manageable.

The Recipes

Crepes Benedict

servings 2 **prep time** 2 minutes
cooking time 8 minutes

4	slices turkey bacon, *Butterball*®
2	10-inch prepared crepes, *Mrs. Frieda*®
4	eggs
2	tablespoons butter
	Salt and pepper
1	can (4-ounce) hollandaise sauce, *Aunt Penny's*®

1. Prepare bacon according to package instructions. Place crepes in plastic wrap and heat in microwave on high for 20 seconds. Whisk eggs in a bowl.

2. In a medium skillet, melt butter over medium heat. Add eggs and stir constantly until light and fluffy, about 2 minutes. Season eggs to taste with salt and pepper.

3. Place hollandaise sauce into a cup and microwave on high about 45 seconds, stirring every 15 seconds. Season sauce to taste with salt and pepper. Set aside.

4. Place 1 crepe on each breakfast plate. Spoon half the scrambled eggs into the center of each crepe and top with 2 bacon slices. Roll up enchilada-style. Top each crepe with 3 tablespoons of hollandaise sauce and serve.

French Apple-Raisin Sandwiches

servings 2 **prep time** 5 minutes
cooking time 8 minutes

French toast has always been one of my favorite breakfast foods. This recipe is especially good because the bread becomes perfectly crunchy around the edges and mildly toasty through the center, while the apple filling adds a soft and sweet accompaniment. Adding syrup makes this breakfast truly decadent.

2	eggs
¼	cup whole milk
¼	teaspoon ground cinnamon, *McCormick*®
4	slices raisin bread, *Wonder*®
½	cup prepared apple pie filling, *Comstock*®
1	tablespoon butter
	Additional butter
	Powdered sugar, *C&H* (optional)

1. In a large baking dish, whisk eggs, milk, and cinnamon. Set aside.

2. Make 2 sandwiches with the bread and apple pie filling. Place sandwiches into egg mixture. Let soak until egg mixture is completely absorbed into the bread, turning sandwiches over occasionally, about 3 minutes.

3. On a griddle over medium-low heat, melt 1 tablespoon of butter. Cook sandwiches on the griddle until brown and heated through, about 4 minutes per side. Cut each sandwich in half.

4. Transfer to plates and serve with additional butter. Top with powdered sugar (optional).

Huevos Rancheros

servings 4 **prep time** 5 minutes
cooking time 12 minutes

This is my all-time favorite breakfast. My nephew Scottie and I have a great time making it, and we always use a fun cookie-cutter shape to cut the tortillas, such as a coyote, cactus, or cowboy hat.

4	burrito-size (10-inch) flour tortillas, *Mission*®
1	can (16-ounce) low-fat refried black beans, *Rosarita*®
2	tablespoons diced green chiles, *Ortega*®
½	cup salsa, *Pace*®
2	tablespoons chopped fresh cilantro
8	eggs
¼	cup shredded sharp cheddar cheese, *Kraft*®
2	green onions, thinly sliced
4	tablespoons sour cream

1. Preheat oven to 400 degrees F. Using cookie cutters, cut tortillas into shapes and place onto a foil-covered baking sheet. Bake until slightly browned, about 4 minutes per side.

2. Meanwhile, combine beans, green chiles, salsa, and cilantro in a medium saucepan. Bring to a simmer over medium heat, stirring occasionally, about 4 minutes. Remove from heat.

3. In a nonstick skillet, cook eggs over-easy or sunny-side up.

4. Divide bean mixture among 4 plates. Place 2 cooked eggs next to the beans on each plate. Arrange the baked tortillas in beans; sprinkle with cheese and green onions. Top with a tablespoon of sour cream.

Morning Glory
Fondue

servings 6 **prep time** 7 minutes
cooking time 8 minutes

This fondue is fabulous! I get so many compliments on this breakfast. It's truly original and quite delicious—an interesting new take on an old favorite. If you're serving it as a dish for a weekend brunch, place it at the center of your table as the focal point of the meal—it's that special.

2	packages (8 ounces each) cream cheese, *Philadelphia*®
1	cup sour cream
2	tablespoons all-purpose flour, *Pillsbury*®
1	tablespoon Dijon mustard, *French's*®
1	cup brut champagne, *Cook's*®
6	ounces smoked salmon, chopped, *Lasco*®
10	cherry tomatoes, quartered
4	hard-boiled eggs, peeled and coarsely chopped
6	English muffins, toasted and cut into 1-inch pieces, *Thomas'*®
3	bagels (plain, water, or egg), halved lengthwise, cut into 1-inch pieces, toasted

1. In a large bowl, using an electric mixer, beat cream cheese, sour cream, flour, and mustard until well blended.

2. Bring champagne to a boil in a medium heavy saucepan over medium-high heat. Reduce heat to medium-low. Gradually whisk cheese mixture into champagne, stirring until cheese melts and mixture is smooth. Stir in salmon, tomatoes, and eggs.

3. Transfer fondue to fondue pot or bowl and keep warm. Serve hot with warmed English muffins and bagel pieces for dipping.

Pumpkin Cinnamon Pancakes

servings 2 **prep time** 5 minutes
cooking time 6 minutes

If you're a pumpkin lover like me, I've got your number—six that is! This stack of six pancakes is every pumpkin fan's dream. This idea came to me on a fall trip to New York. It was "pumpkin everything" at the Regency Hotel, and the pumpkin pancakes were the best I'd ever tasted—so here's my Semi-Homemade® version for you to enjoy! I'd love to hear what you think. (See page 240.)

Pecan Syrup
1   cup maple-flavored pancake syrup, *Log Cabin Original Syrup®*
5   tablespoons chopped pecans, toasted, *Diamond®*

Pancakes
1   cup buttermilk pancake mix, *Aunt Jemima®*
2/3 cup cold water
1/3 cup canned pumpkin, *Libby's®*
1/2 teaspoon ground cinnamon, *McCormick®*
1/8 teaspoon ground ginger, *McCormick®*
     Nonstick vegetable cooking spray, *PAM®*
     Butter, room temperature

Pecan Syrup Preparation
1. Combine maple syrup and pecans in a small microwave-safe bowl. Heat in microwave on high until hot, about 25 seconds. Set pecan syrup aside and keep warm.

Pancakes Preparation
2. In a medium bowl, whisk pancake mix, water, pumpkin, cinnamon, and ginger until just blended (do not overmix; batter should be lumpy).

3. Spray a heavy griddle with nonstick spray and heat griddle over medium heat. Spoon 2 tablespoons batter onto griddle to form each pancake. Cook for 2 minutes or until bubbles appear, then turn pancakes over and cook 2 minutes longer. Transfer pancakes to plates. Top with butter and warm pecan syrup.

English Crown
Scramble

servings 6 **prep time** 5 minutes
cooking time 15 minutes

Mornay Sauce

2	tablespoons butter
1¹/₂	tablespoons all-purpose flour, *Pillsbury®*
1¹/₄	cups whole milk
¹/₄	teaspoon salt
³/₄	cup shredded Swiss cheese, *Sargento®*
¹/₂	cup shredded Parmesan cheese, *Kraft®*

Egg Pastry Crowns

6	frozen puff pastry shells, *Pepperidge Farm®*
6	eggs, lightly beaten
¹/₄	cup whole milk
1	teaspoon vegetable oil, *Wesson®*
1	tablespoon butter
	Salt and pepper
2	tablespoons chopped fresh chives

Mornay Sauce Preparation

1. In medium heavy saucepan, melt butter over medium heat. Add flour and whisk until mixture is smooth, about 1 minute. Whisk in milk and salt. Whisk until mixture thickens slightly, about 2 minutes. Gradually whisk in cheeses. Stir until mixture is smooth and begins to bubble, stirring constantly, about 5 minutes. Cover and keep warm.

Egg Pastry Crowns Preparation

2. Meanwhile, preheat oven to 400 degrees F. Place pastry shells on a cookie sheet and bake for 12 minutes or until golden on top.

3. Whisk eggs and milk in a large bowl to blend. Place a large nonstick skillet over medium heat. Add oil and butter to skillet. When the butter foams, add the egg mixture. Stir continuously with a rubber spatula until eggs are light and fluffy, about 2 minutes. Season to taste with salt and pepper.

4. Remove tops and hollow out pastry shells. Divide scrambled eggs among pastries. Top each with 2 to 3 tablespoons of Mornay Sauce. Sprinkle with chives and serve.

Storage and Leftovers: Mornay Sauce can be stored for up to 2 days. Cover tightly and refrigerate. Reheat over low heat, stirring constantly.

Country Biscuits and Gravy

servings 4 **prep time** 5 minutes
cooking time 12 minutes

Nothing is better than old-fashioned biscuits, hot or cold. Then when they're smothered in gravy—look out. Whether you're making this wonderful down-home breakfast for one or ten, it's quick and easy, and I promise it will hit the spot.

8	ounces (bulk) pork sausage, crumbled, *Jimmy Dean*®
1	can (10.5-ounce) white sauce, *Aunt Penny's*®
³/₄	cup whole milk
	Salt and pepper
1	container (10.2-ounce) prepared buttermilk biscuit dough, *Pillsbury*® *Grands!*®

1. In a small skillet over medium heat, saute sausage until thoroughly cooked, about 4 minutes. Add white sauce and milk. Bring to a simmer. Cover and simmer 2 minutes to blend flavors. Season to taste with salt and pepper.

2. Meanwhile, bake biscuits according to package instructions. Cut baked biscuits in half and place two halves on each plate. Spoon sausage gravy generously over tops of biscuits and serve.

Storage and Leftovers: Store biscuits in a resealable bag at room temperature for up to 2 days. Cover gravy tightly and store in refrigerator for up to 2 days. To reheat, combine gravy and reduced-fat milk (as needed) in a saucepan over low heat, stirring constantly until warm.

Date-Bran Carrot
Muffins

servings 12 muffins **prep time** 5 minutes
cooking time 20 minutes

	Nonstick vegetable cooking spray, *PAM*®
1	package (16.6-ounce) date muffin mix, *Pillsbury*®
1	cup wheat bran
1	cup whole milk
1	egg
1	cup shredded carrots, *Mann's*®
³/₄	cup chopped pitted dates, (dates may be available already chopped), *Sunsweet*®

1. Preheat oven to 400 degrees F. Line 12 muffin tins with muffin papers or spray with nonstick spray.

2. In a medium bowl, stir muffin mix, bran, milk, and egg until just blended. Fold in carrots and dates (do not overmix; the batter should be lumpy).

3. Divide batter equally among muffin tins. Bake until a toothpick inserted into muffin centers comes out clean, about 20 minutes. Serve warm or at room temperature.

Storage and Leftovers: Store in an airtight container for up to 2 days.

Eggs in a Nest

servings 4 **prep time** 8 minutes
cooking time 8 minutes

Cheez Wiz? Cheez Whiz®! Cheez Whiz®? Holy Cow! Everyone who's anyone in the food business has told me that this book will receive the worst reviews if I include Cheez Whiz® in any of my recipes! But the consistency is the perfect texture for this recipe and it tastes great on eggs. So my apologies to the food critics and purists—but please just give this a try and I promise you'll be saying "Holy Cow" because this recipe is so wonderful!

	Nonstick vegetable cooking spray, *PAM®*
6	eggs
½	teaspoon ground black pepper, *McCormick®*
½	teaspoon seasoned salt, *Lawry's®*
2	tablespoons butter
4	slices light whole wheat bread, *Wonder®*
8	teaspoons cheese dip, *Kraft® Cheez Whiz®*

1. Preheat oven to 325 degrees F. Spray four 1-cup ovenproof custard or dessert cups with nonstick spray.

2. In a large bowl, whisk eggs, pepper, and seasoned salt until foamy.

3. In a large nonstick skillet over medium heat, melt 1 tablespoon of the butter. Add egg mixture and stir constantly about 2 minutes or until eggs are almost set.

4. Spread remaining 1 tablespoon butter over one side of each bread slice (this prevents eggs from making the bread soggy). Place 1 bread slice, buttered side up, into each cup, pressing to fit. Spoon 1 teaspoon cheese dip on top of each bread slice. Divide eggs equally among cups. Spoon 1 teaspoon of cheese dip over top of each.

5. Bake until cheese is melted, about 5 minutes. Serve hot.

Note: Garnish with shredded cheese and chopped tomatoes, if desired.

Strawberry-Banana Bread Pudding

servings 10 **prep time** 5 minutes **cooking time** 50 minutes **cooling time** 15 minutes

	Nonstick vegetable cooking spray, *PAM*®
1	container (16-ounce) frozen sweetened sliced strawberries (about 2 cups), thawed and drained (reserve syrup; set aside)
1	package (13.9-ounce) banana quick bread mix, *Betty Crocker*®
2	eggs
3	tablespoons canola oil, *Wesson*®
1	container (8-ounce) mixed berry yogurt, *Colombo*®
1	cup plain yogurt, *Colombo*®

1. Preheat oven to 375 degrees F. Spray bottom of an 8×4×3-inch loaf pan with nonstick spray.

2. Stir 1¼ cups strawberries, banana bread mix, eggs, and oil in a large bowl to blend. Transfer batter to prepared pan.

3. Bake until a toothpick inserted into center of bread comes out clean, about 50 minutes. Cool 15 minutes in pan. Remove bread from pan.

4. Meanwhile, stir remaining ¾ cup strawberries (with syrup), berry yogurt, and plain yogurt in medium bowl to blend. Cover and refrigerate until ready to serve.

5. Cut bread crosswise into 10 slices. Transfer slices to plates. Top each with a dollop of yogurt mixture and serve.

Lunch

Lighter, smaller portions eaten at noon can be as appetizing and satisfying as dinner. Lunches shared with coworkers, friends, or family are always a midday delight. Looking back on my childhood, one of the highlights of my day was the delectable surprise awaiting me at lunchtime. Little did I know how necessary lunch is toward maintaining a healthy attitude and high energy level. Now, lunch is about taking a little personal time to enjoy a meal, catch up, and catch my breath.

Often lunch can seem uneventful and humdrum, especially when it's the same old selection in the fridge, or when there is nothing appealing at the local restaurants, delis, or fast-food chains. Semi-Homemade® lunches will entice the pickiest of palates and put the pizzazz back into your noonday breaks. You will find recipes suitable for weekdays or weekends, intimate lunches, or playtime pow-wows.

Whether you want to eat light, are feeling famished, or just want something healthful to nosh, there is much to choose from in this chapter. Best of all, each recipe is quick to make and tastes great whether you're lunching at home or the office.

The Recipes

Pepper Peach
Chicken Skewers

servings 24 skewers **prep time** 30 minutes
cooking time 12 minutes

It was hard to decide where to place this recipe. These Pepper Peach Chicken Skewers could easily be served as appetizers (they're perfect for guests) or for dinner (just use longer skewers and more chicken and peaches). But lunches fill the bill since I eat these mostly on Saturday or Sunday afternoons. Feel free to serve them anytime; they'll always be welcome. By the way, I think you'll be happily surprised at how well pepper and peach complement each other.

24	small wooden skewers (6-inch)
1	tablespoon olive oil, *Bertolli*®
1	tablespoon lemon juice, or *ReaLemon*®
2	teaspoons bottled minced garlic, *McCormick*®
1	teaspoon ground black pepper, *McCormick*®
3/4	teaspoon ground cumin, *McCormick*®
4	boneless, skinless chicken breasts, each cut into 6 cubes
2	firm ripe fresh peaches, pitted, each cut into 12 cubes
	Salt

1. Soak wood skewers in water for 10 minutes.

2. In a medium bowl, mix oil, lemon juice, garlic, pepper, and cumin for marinade. Toss chicken cubes in the marinade. Cover and refrigerate for 20 minutes.

3. Preheat broiler. Place 1 chicken cube and 1 peach cube onto each skewer. Sprinkle with salt. Place on a broiler pan. Broil until chicken is cooked through and beginning to brown. Turn skewers halfway through cooking to brown on all sides, about 12 minutes total.

4. Arrange skewers on platter and serve immediately.

Black Bean
Quesadilla

servings 2 **prep time** 5 minutes
cooking time 15 minutes

Mexican food is my favorite food of all. I could eat it morning, noon, and night. It's true. This recipe is quick and delicious and is one of my favorites. It's so fast to make too!

2	burrito-size (10-inch) flour tortillas, *Mission*®
1	cup canned refried low-fat black beans, *Rosarito*®
1	cup chunky salsa, *Pace*®
1	cup Mexican-style shredded cheese, *Kraft*®
$^1/_2$	cup prepared guacamole (refrigerated section)
2	tablespoons sour cream

1. Preheat oven to 400 degrees F. Lay one tortilla on a clean work surface. Spread the beans evenly over the tortilla. Spoon $^3/_4$ cup of the salsa over the beans, then sprinkle with the cheese. Top with the second tortilla.

2. Place the quesadilla on a foil-covered cookie sheet. Bake for approximately 15 minutes or until the cheese is melted and the top is crisp and brown. Meanwhile, swirl the guacamole and sour cream together in a small bowl.

3. Cut the quesadilla into 4 equal portions and transfer to a plate. Serve with the guacamole mixture and remaining $^1/_4$ cup of salsa.

Storage and Leftovers: Cover tightly and refrigerate; store for up to 1 day. Reheat in a 400-degree oven for about 10 minutes or until hot.

Southwestern Turkey Chili and Corn Bread

servings 2 **prep time** 5 minutes
cooking time 25 minutes

Canned chili and stew carried me through my college years. I put it in omelets, poured it over biscuits, and sometimes would eat it right out of the can. It was hearty, satisfying, and affordable. At the time I didn't even think about what the meat content might be—thank goodness, because I would have starved! But here's a way to tantalize your taste buds with an all-time favorite using vegetarian-like products and your own fresh meat. This chili is fantastic every day and fabulous for football Sundays. Let me know what your friends and family think! (See page 240.)

Corn Bread
	Nonstick vegetable cooking spray, *PAM*®
1	can (11-ounce) Mexicorn, *Green Giant*®
1	egg
1	package (8^1/2-ounce) corn muffin mix, *Jiffy*®

Chili
10	ounces lean ground turkey, crumbled
1	tablespoon all-purpose flour, *Pillsbury*®
1	tablespoon olive oil, *Bertolli*®
1	can (15.5-ounce) spicy black beans, *S&W Regional Recipe: San Antonio Beans*®
1	can (14^1/2-ounce) stewed tomatoes, Mexican recipe style, *S&W*®
	Sour cream, chopped fresh cilantro, chopped red onion

Corn Bread Preparation

1. Preheat oven to 400 degrees F. Spray 8×8×2-inch baking pan with nonstick spray.

2. Drain liquid from Mexicorn, reserving 2 tablespoons liquid. Place the reserved 2 tablespoons liquid in a medium bowl. Add egg to liquid and whisk to blend. Stir in Mexicorn. Add corn muffin mix; stir just until blended.

3. Transfer mixture to prepared pan. Bake until a toothpick inserted into center of corn bread comes out clean, about 20 minutes.

Chili Preparation

4. Meanwhile, in a resealable plastic bag, toss turkey with flour until flour is absorbed into meat. Heat oil in a wide 2-quart pot over medium heat. Saute the turkey until brown, about 5 minutes.

5. Add beans and tomatoes. Simmer over medium-low heat until chili is slightly thick, about 8 minutes.

6. Spoon chili into bowls. Top with sour cream, cilantro, and onion. Serve hot with corn bread.

Storage and Leftovers: Cover tightly and store corn bread at room temperature for up to 3 days. Cover tightly and store chili in refrigerator for up to 3 days. Reheat over medium heat.

Gnocchi Dippers

servings 4 **prep time** 4 minutes
cooking time 10 minutes

1	package (9-ounce) gnocchi (dry pasta section), *Alessi*®, or cheese tortellini pasta, *Rosetto*®
2	teaspoons olive oil, *Bertolli*®
¼	onion, minced
2	teaspoons bottled minced garlic, *McCormick*®
1	package (8-ounce) cheese product, *Kraft*® *Velveeta*®
½	cup low-fat milk
¼	teaspoon hot sauce, *Tabasco*®
8	teaspoons light sour cream
	Fresh thyme sprigs (optional)

1. Prepare gnocchi according to package instructions.

2. Heat oil in a medium saucepan over medium heat. Saute onion and garlic in oil until onion is tender, about 2 minutes. Add the cheese product, milk, and hot sauce. Stir until sauce is smooth and cheese has completely melted, about 4 minutes.

3. Fold cooked gnocchi into sauce. Transfer gnocchi and sauce to 4 bowls. Top each serving with 2 teaspoons sour cream and garnish with thyme sprigs (optional). Serve immediately.

Storage and Leftovers: Cover tightly and store in refrigerator for up to 2 days. To reheat, combine gnocchi and low-fat milk (as needed) in a saucepan over medium heat, stirring frequently until warm.

Prosciutto and
Goat Cheese Pizza

servings 2 **prep time** 6 minutes
cooking time 12 minutes

I love this pizza, love this pizza, am in love with this pizza! It's delicious, and once you put the first bite in your mouth, you'll be in love with it too! It's simple, quick, and fun to make.

1	fully baked thin pizza crust (10-ounce), *Boboli*®
½	cup marinara sauce, *Boboli*®
1	cup shredded mozzarella cheese, *Kraft*®
1	package (3-ounce) thinly sliced prosciutto (deli section), *Citterio*®
1	ounce soft fresh goat cheese, coarsely crumbled
2	tablespoons chopped fresh basil

1. Preheat oven to 425 degrees F.

2. Lay pizza crust on a foil-covered pizza pan or cookie sheet. Spread sauce evenly over pizza crust. Sprinkle mozzarella cheese over crust, leaving a 1-inch border around edge. Arrange prosciutto on top of cheese. Sprinkle goat cheese over prosciutto.

3. Bake until prosciutto is crisp and cheeses are melted, about 12 minutes. Sprinkle basil over pizza. Cut pizza into 6 slices and serve.

Storage and Leftovers: Cover tightly and store in refrigerator for up to 2 days. Reheat in a 425-degree oven for about 10 minutes or until warm.

Curried Bow Tie
Salad

servings 4 **prep time** 10 minutes
cooking time 5 minutes **cooling time** 15 minutes

¾   cup sour cream
2   teaspoons curry powder, *McCormick*®
2   cans (8 ounces each) pineapple chunks, drained, *Dole*®
1   ripe medium avocado, peeled, pitted, and sliced
1   medium red apple, cored and sliced
8   ounces bow tie pasta/farfalle (half of a 16-ounce
         package), *De Cecco*®
     Salt

1. In a large bowl, mix sour cream and curry powder to blend. Fold in pineapple, avocado, and apple.

2. Meanwhile, cook pasta in a pot of boiling salted water until just tender, about 5 minutes. Drain. Rinse pasta under cold water to cool, then let drain well. Fold pasta into sour cream mixture. Refrigerate until cold, about 15 minutes. Season salad to taste with salt and serve.

Note: Salad can be served on a bed of shredded red cabbage or on fresh baby spinach.

Storage and Leftovers: Cover tightly and store in refrigerator for up to 1 day.

Beefy Stew

servings 4 **prep time** 10 minutes
cooking time 35 minutes

When making stew, I like to use canned vegetable soup and then add my own choice of fresh meat to it. To me, it tastes much better than ordinary canned stew and it's fresher. This stew recipe makes a wonderfully hearty meal. Double or triple the recipe and keep it in the fridge—it makes great leftovers!

1	sheet frozen puff pastry, thawed, cut into four 4-inch rounds, *Pepperidge Farm*®
1½	pounds beef cube steak, cut into 1-inch pieces
	Salt and pepper
2	tablespoons all-purpose flour, *Pillsbury*®
¼	cup vegetable oil, *Wesson*®
1	can (14-ounce) reduced-sodium beef broth, *Swanson*®
1	jar (24-ounce) country vegetable soup, *Campbell's*®

1. Position rack in center of oven and preheat to 425 degrees F. Arrange puff pastry rounds on a large heavy cookie sheet. Bake pastry rounds until puffed, golden brown, and cooked through, about 12 minutes. Set aside and keep warm.

2. Meanwhile, sprinkle beef with salt and pepper. Toss beef with flour in a large bowl to coat. Heat oil in a large heavy casserole over medium-high heat. Add a third of the beef to oil and saute until brown, about 5 minutes. Using a slotted spoon, transfer beef to bowl. Repeat with remaining beef.

3. Add beef broth and bring to a simmer, stirring to loosen browned bits on bottom. Return all beef and any accumulated juices to casserole. Add soup and simmer, uncovered, until liquid thickens slightly and beef is tender, about 15 minutes.

4. Divide stew equally among 4 bowls. Top each with a warm puff pastry round and serve.

Storage and Leftovers: Store puff pastries in a resealable bag at room temperature for up to 2 days. Cover tightly and store Beefy Stew in refrigerator for up to 2 days. To reheat, combine Beefy Stew and ¼ cup water in a saucepan over medium heat, stirring frequently until warm.

Salad Chinois

servings 4
prep time 10 minutes

This salad is a sleeper! It's never the first thing anyone ever makes, but I guarantee once you try it you'll be hooked. Here's a little secret: I make the dressing and serve it as a dip—it's the best—you'll want to put it on everything.

Dressing
²/₃	cup mayonnaise, *Best Foods*® or *Hellmann's*®
2	tablespoons reduced-sodium soy sauce, *Kikkoman*®
1	teaspoon ground ginger, *McCormick*®

Salad
1	can (10-ounce) premium chunk chicken breast, drained and chilled, *Swanson*®
2	cups coleslaw mix (shredded cabbage and carrots, without sauce), *Ready Pac*®
1	can (14-ounce) chow mein vegetables, drained and chilled, *Chun King*®
1	bag (5-ounce) prepared green salad, *Fresh Express*®
1	can (5-ounce) chow mein noodles, *La Choy*®
1	can (11-ounce) mandarin orange segments, drained and chilled, *Dole*®

Dressing Preparation
1. In a small bowl, blend mayonnaise, soy sauce, and ginger.

Salad Preparation
2. In a large bowl, toss chicken, coleslaw mix, and drained chow mein vegetables until well mixed. Toss chicken mixture with enough dressing to coat well.

3. Line 4 bowls or plates with a small amount of green salad. Spoon chicken mixture on top of green salad. Garnish with noodles and orange segments before serving.

Note: Serve with fresh melon skewers or sliced fresh pineapple.

Storage and Leftovers: Cover tightly and store in refrigerator for up to 1 day.

Six-Cheese Tortellini

servings 4 **prep time** 5 minutes
cooking time 12 minutes

2   tablespoons butter
1   cup whole milk
¼   cup cheese dip, *Kraft® Cheez Whiz®*
1   package (8-ounce) shredded Six-Cheese Italian Blend
          (mozzarella, smoked provolone, Parmesan, Romano, fontina,
          and Asiago cheeses), *Sargento®*
⅛   teaspoon cayenne pepper, *McCormick®*
2   packages (9 ounces each) fresh cheese tortellini
          (refrigerated section), *Rosetto®*

1. Melt butter in a large heavy saucepan over medium heat. Add milk and bring to a simmer. Whisk in cheese dip. Gradually whisk in shredded cheeses. Stir until cheeses melt and mixture begins to bubble, about 5 minutes. Whisk in cayenne.

2. Meanwhile, cook tortellini in a pot of boiling salted water until just tender, about 4 minutes. Drain. Add tortellini to cheese sauce. Toss to coat. Divide tortellini and sauce equally among 4 pasta bowls and serve.

Note: Can be made 1 day ahead. Transfer tortellini and sauce to a 2-quart baking dish. Cover and bake until heated through, about 25 minutes.

Storage and Leftovers: Cover tightly and store in refrigerator for up to 2 days. To reheat, combine tortellini and whole milk (as needed) in a saucepan over medium heat, stirring frequently until warm.

Dinner

Dinner should be seen as a celebration that ends another productive day. It's a time to reflect and share ideas, new happenings, and current events. It's also a time for you and yours to relax and unwind, a time for families to share and bond while reinforcing the security and stability of home. Dinner should be a pleasure—a time to laugh, have fun, and enjoy one another's company. It shouldn't be yet another stressful "to-do" on your list. Preparing dinner can be easy and satisfying with Semi-Homemade® recipes.

Many of us have dinner on the run. For you domestic goddesses, bad habits are easily formed as you constantly try to squeeze your families' dinner in between soccer practice, homework, and last-minute errands. For you corporate devotees, takeout and order-in at the office are commonplace when trying to meet demanding deadlines (I know!). Regardless, both scenarios are unhealthful and rob everyone of the important downtime and pleasure of a good meal. Semi-Homemade® dinners are simple to make and give you more time to enjoy yourself and others without sacrificing taste or nutrition. Bon appétit.

The Recipes

Dijon Chicken and Mushrooms

servings 4 **prep time** 7 minutes
cooking time 25 minutes

Anyone who's ever eaten with me would describe me as one of the pickiest eaters they've ever seen, and chicken has never been my favorite food. However, several years ago I had one of the most amazing meals ever, Dijon Chicken and Mushrooms. It took me nearly two years to perfect this recipe and then two minutes to clean my plate.

4	boneless, skinless chicken breasts (about 6 ounces each)
	Salt and pepper
2	tablespoons butter
8	white button mushrooms, finely chopped
1	can (10-ounce) condensed fat-free cream of mushroom soup, *Campbell's*®
½	cup canned chicken broth, *Swanson*®
¼	cup Dijon mustard, *French's*®
2	tablespoons deli-style brown mustard, *French's*®
1	tomato, diced
¼	cup frozen cut corn kernels, thawed, *Green Giant*®
¼	cup chopped fresh chives

1. Sprinkle chicken with salt and pepper. Melt butter in a large heavy skillet over medium-high heat. Add chicken and cook until just brown, about 4 minutes per side. Transfer chicken to plate.

2. Add mushrooms to the same skillet and saute until tender, about 3 minutes. Whisk in soup, broth, and mustards. Bring sauce to a simmer.

3. Return chicken to skillet and submerge into sauce completely. Reduce heat to medium-low. Cover and cook until soup bubbles thickly and chicken is cooked through, about 10 minutes.

4. Transfer chicken to plates and spoon sauce over the top. Sprinkle with tomato, corn, and chives. Serve hot.

Steak Pinwheels with Sun-Dried Tomato Stuffing and Rosemary Mashed Potatoes

servings 4 to 6 **prep time** 12 minutes
cooking time 50 minutes

Steak

1²/₃	cups canned beef broth, *Swanson*®
³/₄	cup ready-to-use julienne sun-dried tomatoes (not packed in oil), *Frieda's*®
¹/₄	cup butter
1	package (6.6-ounce) stuffing mix, *Stove Top*® (flavor optional)
1	1¹/₄-pound skirt steak
	Salt and pepper

Rosemary Mashed Potatoes

2	packages (11 ounces each) refrigerated prepared mashed potatoes, *Simply Potatoes*®
6	tablespoons butter
¹/₄	cup whole milk
2	teaspoons finely chopped fresh rosemary
	Salt and pepper

Steak Preparation

1. Bring broth, sun-dried tomatoes, and butter to a boil in a medium saucepan. Stir in contents of stuffing mix pouch. Cover saucepan and remove from heat. Let stand for 5 minutes. Fluff the stuffing with fork. Cool stuffing.

2. Preheat oven to 425 degrees F. Lay steak flat onto clean work surface. Sprinkle steak with salt and pepper. Cover steak evenly with stuffing. Roll up steak lengthwise to create a pinwheel effect, enclosing stuffing completely. Skewer seam with toothpicks. Place the steak roll, seam side down, onto a foil-covered cookie sheet. Sprinkle roll with salt and pepper. Roast until steak is golden brown and cooked through, about 40 minutes.

Rosemary Mashed Potatoes Preparation

3. Meanwhile, peel back corners of potato packages. Warm potatoes in microwave according to package instructions. Mix in butter, milk, and rosemary. Season potatoes to taste with salt and pepper.

Note: May be served with my More-Than-Meatloaf Gravy (recipe found in Gravies and Sauces chapter, see page 209).

Lemon Turkey
Cutlets

servings 4 **prep time** 8 minutes
cooking time 12 minutes

1 1/2	pounds refrigerated boneless turkey cutlets, *The Turkey Store*®
	Salt and pepper
1/3	cup all-purpose flour, *Pillsbury*®
1	egg, lightly beaten
2	tablespoons fresh lemon juice, or *ReaLemon*®
1	cup Italian-style bread crumbs, *Progresso*®
2	tablespoons finely chopped onion
1/3	cup vegetable oil, *Wesson*®

1. Rinse cutlets with cold water and pat dry with paper towels. Sprinkle cutlets with salt and pepper.

2. Place flour in a medium bowl. In another medium bowl, combine egg and lemon juice. In a third medium bowl, combine bread crumbs and onion.

3. Heat oil in a large skillet over medium-high heat. Working in batches, dip cutlets into flour, then egg mixture, and then bread crumb mixture. Place cutlets in hot oil and cook until brown, about 3 minutes per side.

Note: May be served with my Creamy Mustard Sauce (recipe found in Gravies and Sauces chapter, see page 206).

Sweet-and-Sour Pork Kabobs with Fried Rice

servings 4 **prep time** 30 minutes
cooking time 20 minutes

Kabobs

1/3	cup sweet-and-sour sauce, *Dynasty*®
1/4	cup pineapple juice from canned pineapple, *Dole*®
2	tablespoons soy sauce, *Kikkoman*®
1	garlic clove, minced
1	teaspoon peeled and minced fresh ginger
1	pound pork tenderloin, cut crosswise into 12 equal pieces
4	button mushrooms
4	cherry tomatoes
1	small zucchini, cut crosswise into 4 equal pieces
1/2	green bell pepper, quartered
1/2	red bell pepper, quartered
1/2	can (8-ounce) pineapple chunks, drained, *Dole*®
4	10-inch wood skewers, soaked in water 10 minutes

Fried Rice

1	package (6.25-ounce) fried rice, *Rice-A-Roni*®
1	tablespoon butter
1 1/2	cups water
2	tablespoons soy sauce, *Kikkoman*®
1/3	cup frozen peas and carrots, thawed, *Green Giant*®
1/4	cup frozen cut corn kernels, thawed, *Green Giant*®

Kabob Preparation

1. In a small bowl, mix sweet-and-sour sauce, pineapple juice, soy sauce, garlic, and ginger. Set marinade aside. Place pork into a medium bowl. In another medium bowl, place vegetables and pineapple. Distribute marinade evenly between the 2 bowls and toss pork to coat. Refrigerate at least 15 minutes or up to 8 hours.

2. Preheat broiler. Alternate pork, vegetables, and pineapple evenly on 4 skewers. Place skewers onto a broiler pan and broil until pork is cooked through and beginning to brown, turning skewers halfway through cooking, about 5 minutes per side.

Fried Rice Preparation

3. Meanwhile, combine rice-vermicelli mix from fried rice package (reserve seasonings) and butter in a large heavy skillet. Saute over medium heat until vermicelli is golden brown, about 2 minutes. Gradually add the 1 1/2 cups water, soy sauce, and special seasonings from fried rice package. Bring to a boil. Cover skillet. Reduce heat to low. Simmer until rice is tender, about 15 minutes.

4. Remove skillet from heat. Sprinkle peas and carrots and corn over rice mixture. Cover and let rice stand 5 minutes. Using fork, fluff rice and mix in peas, carrots, and corn. Serve with Kabobs.

Mushroom Steak and Sweet Mash

servings 4 **prep time** 5 minutes
cooking time 40 minutes

Mushroom Steak
4	beef cube steaks (about 4 ounces each)
	Salt and pepper
$\frac{1}{2}$	cup all-purpose flour, *Pillsbury*®
$\frac{1}{4}$	cup vegetable oil, *Wesson*®
2	cans (14 ounces each) beef broth, *Swanson*®
1	can (10$\frac{3}{4}$-ounce) condensed golden mushroom soup, *Campbell's*®
1	white onion, cut into $\frac{1}{4}$-inch slices and separated into rings

Sweet Mash
1	can (15-ounce) cut sweet potatoes, drained and rinsed, *Princella*®
$\frac{1}{2}$	cup whole milk
4	tablespoons butter
2	tablespoons golden brown sugar, *C&H*®
	Salt and pepper
1	package (11-ounce) refrigerated prepared mashed potatoes, *Simply Potatoes*®

Mushroom Steak Preparation
1. Sprinkle steaks generously with salt and pepper. Place flour into large soup plate or pie pan. Dredge steaks in flour, coating completely. Heat oil in a large skillet on medium-high heat. Fry 2 floured steaks in skillet until just brown, about 3 minutes per side. Transfer steaks to paper towel (to drain excess oil). Repeat with remaining steaks.

2. Sprinkle remaining flour from plate into remaining oil in skillet (do not remove pan drippings from skillet). Stir continuously until paste is dark brown, about 3 minutes. Reduce heat to low. Whisk in beef broth. Stir in soup. Return steaks to skillet, submerging in gravy completely. Top with onion rings. Cover and simmer for 20 minutes or until gravy is thick. Season gravy to taste with salt and pepper.

Sweet Mash Preparation
3. Meanwhile, use a fork to mash sweet potatoes in a medium microwave-safe bowl. Mix in $\frac{1}{4}$ cup of the milk, 2 tablespoons of the butter, and the brown sugar. Cover tightly with plastic wrap and cook in microwave on high until hot, about 3 minutes. Season sweet potatoes to taste with salt and pepper. Set aside and keep warm.

4. Peel back corner of mashed potatoes package. Warm potatoes in microwave according to package instructions. Mix in remaining $\frac{1}{4}$ cup milk and 2 tablespoons butter. Season potatoes to taste with salt and pepper.

Presentation
5. Swirl mashed potatoes with sweet potatoes on each plate. Place steak on top of potatoes. Smother steaks with gravy. Garnish with onions and serve.

Tropical Salmon

servings 2 **prep time** 15 minutes
cooking time 20 minutes

When I moved to Los Angeles from Wisconsin, I rented a room in a house from two German men and a Portuguese woman—there is no punch line here. One of the men was a private chef for the rich and famous and shared many of his secret recipes with me. This was one of his favorites, and now I am so happy to be sharing it with you. It's perfect for a romantic evening and will make you look brilliant.

Tropical Rice
1	bag (2-cup) white rice, *Uncle Ben's Boil-in-Bag Rice*®
1/4	cup dried tropical fruit mix, *Sunsweet Fruitlings*®
1/4	cup dry-roasted peanuts, chopped, *Planters*®

Salmon and Chive Sauce
2	tablespoons tartar sauce, *Kraft*®
2	tablespoons sour cream
2	tablespoons fresh lime juice
1	tablespoon Dijon mustard, *French's*®
2	teaspoons chopped fresh chives
1	skinless salmon fillet (12-ounce), cut crosswise into ten 1/2-inch slices
	Fresh dill (optional)

Tropical Rice Preparation
1. Prepare rice according to package instructions, adding dried fruit halfway through cooking time. Remove rice from heat. Mix in nuts. Transfer rice to serving bowl.

Salmon and Chive Sauce Preparation
2. Meanwhile, in a small bowl, mix tartar sauce, sour cream, lime juice, mustard, and chives. Cover chive sauce and refrigerate.

3. Preheat broiler. Divide salmon slices between 2 broilerproof glass or ceramic plates, covering half of each of the plates. Place plates under broiler and cook until salmon is pale pink and flaky, watching salmon carefully so it does not overcook, about 1 minute.

4. Using potholders, carefully remove hot plates. Spoon chive sauce on top of salmon and serve with rice. Garnish with fresh dill (optional).

Speedy
Swedish Meatballs

servings 4 **prep time** 5 minutes
cooking time 15 minutes

I've been to some of the most acclaimed restaurants in the world—and loved every minute. But I must admit I truly love a good old-fashioned smorgasbord. Some of my friends are cringing right now I know—but I find smorgasbord food to be quite good, fun, and a great value. I always go right for the Swedish meatballs. So when creating this book, it was on the top of my list to include my very own Swedish meatball dinner. This version has an upscale twist with the addition of broad egg noodles.

¼   cup vegetable oil, *Wesson®*
2   pounds (32 ounces) frozen beef meatballs, thawed, *Oh Boy®*
2   tablespoons all-purpose flour, *Pillsbury®*
1   can (14-ounce) reduced-sodium beef broth, *Swanson®*
1½   cups whole milk
¼   cup sour cream
1   package (8.8-ounce) egg noodles, *De Cecco®*

1. In a large heavy skillet, heat oil over medium-high heat. Add meatballs and cook until brown, about 8 minutes. Using tongs, transfer meatballs to a bowl.

2. Add flour to skillet and cook 1 minute, scraping up browned bits from bottom of skillet. Stir in broth and milk. Return meatballs to skillet. Simmer until liquid thickens enough to coat meatballs, about 5 minutes. Remove skillet from heat. Stir in sour cream.

3. Meanwhile, cook noodles in a pot of boiling salted water until tender but still firm. Drain. Transfer noodles to a large bowl.

4. Spoon meatballs and sauce over noodles. Serve immediately.

Storage and Leftovers: Cover tightly and store in refrigerator for up to 2 days. To reheat, combine meatballs and whole milk (as needed) in a saucepan over medium heat, stirring frequently, about 10 minutes or until warm. Cook fresh noodles when re-serving.

Noodles Alfredo

servings 2 **prep time** 5 minutes
cooking time 10 minutes

This recipe rocks! It's rich, creamy and absolutely delicious. My sister Cindy turned me on to it and I adore it almost as much as I adore her (love you, Sis).

8	ounces fettuccine (half of 16-ounce package), *De Cecco*®
1½	sticks butter
1	cup whole milk
1	cup grated Parmesan cheese, *Kraft*®
	Salt

1. In a large pot of boiling salted water, cook noodles according to package instructions. Drain.

2. Return noodles to pot and place over low heat. Add butter and milk to noodles and toss until butter is melted. Add cheese and stir just until melted. Remove from heat. Salt to taste. Serve immediately.

Appetizers and Cocktails

Social soirees can be simple, elegant, and inexpensive to pull off when you use shortcuts. I have thrown many a great party—some for five guests, others for 50 guests, even one for 550 guests. And I can tell you, preparation and attitude are everything—even when you're only entertaining for two, be it a romantic gesture or catch-up time with your best friend.

With the right combination of appetizers and cocktails, your gathering will be a guaranteed success. Good food, a fun atmosphere, and stylish presentation are always important, but preparation doesn't need to be elaborate for the results to be tasteful. While everyone will appreciate your hard work, there is no reason why they should know you didn't labor in the kitchen for hours.

With a little organization and simple Semi-Homemade® recipes, you'll have the freedom to sit back, relax, and enjoy yourself and your guests.

The Recipes

Sesame Chicken Drumettes

servings 4 **prep time** 35 minutes
cooking time 25 minutes

There used to be a place on the 3rd Street Promenade in Santa Monica, California, that cooked up the most amazing drumettes—that's all they served. Unbelievable, wonderful drumettes in all sorts of flavors; sesame was my favorite. When they closed shop, I scrambled to create a recipe that could pass as a twin. Full of flavor, the outside is always perfectly crispy, and the inside is tender and juicy.

$^1/_3$ cup teriyaki sauce, **Kikkoman®**
$1^1/_2$ tablespoons dry sherry, **Christian Brothers®**
$1^1/_2$ tablespoons toasted sesame seeds, **Sun Luck®**
$1^1/_4$ pounds chicken drumettes (about 12)
$1^1/_2$ tablespoons barbecue sauce, **KC Masterpiece®**
$1^1/_2$ tablespoons honey, **Sue Bee®**
$^1/_4$ teaspoon oriental sesame oil, **Sun Luck®**

1. In a large resealable plastic bag, combine teriyaki sauce, sherry, and sesame seeds. Add chicken drumettes, turning to coat. Seal bag and refrigerate at least 30 minutes or up to 1 day.

2. Preheat oven to 400 degrees F. Line a cookie sheet with foil. Using tongs, transfer drumettes to cookie sheet. Discard marinade. Bake until drumettes are golden brown, about 15 minutes.

3. Mix barbecue sauce, honey, and sesame oil in a small bowl. Brush drumettes with honey mixture and bake 5 minutes. Turn drumettes and brush with honey mixture and bake 5 minutes longer. Serve hot.

Storage and Leftovers: Cover tightly and store in refrigerator for up to 2 days. Reheat in a 400-degree oven for 20 minutes or until hot.

Pan-Fried Dumplings

makes 12 dumplings **prep time** 15 minutes
cooking time 18 minutes

2 teaspoons soy sauce, *Kikkoman*®
1 teaspoon hot Chinese-style mustard, *Sun Luck*®
$^{1}/_{2}$ teaspoon minced fresh garlic, *McCormick*®
$^{1}/_{2}$ teaspoon oriental sesame oil, *Sun Luck*®
1 can (14-ounce) chow mein vegetables,
　　 rinsed and drained very well, *Chun King*®
24 square wonton wrappers, *Dynasty*®
$^{1}/_{2}$ cup canola oil, *Wesson*®
　　 Toasted white sesame seeds, *Sun Luck*®
　　 Black sesame seeds, *Wel-Pac*®
　　 Dipping sauces: soy sauce, sweet-and-sour sauce,
　　 and hot Chinese-style mustard

1. Preheat oven to 350 degrees F. Blend soy sauce, Chinese-style mustard, garlic, and sesame oil in a food processor. Add vegetables. Using on/off function, pulse until vegetables are just minced. Drain excess liquid from vegetable mixture.

2. Arrange 12 wonton wrappers on work surface. Lightly brush edges of wrappers with water. Spoon 1 tablespoon vegetable mixture into center of each wrapper. Top with remaining wonton wrappers, pressing to enclose filling completely. Using ravioli cutter or sharp knife, cut edges of wontons.

3. Heat canola oil in large heavy skillet over medium heat. Working in batches, fry dumplings until just golden, about 1 minute per side.

4. Arrange fried dumplings, rounded sides up, on a large cookie sheet. Bake until dumplings are golden brown, about 10 minutes. Transfer dumplings to serving tray. Sprinkle with sesame seeds. Serve with dipping sauces.

Note: Once assembled, dumplings can be frozen and cooked as directed.

Chorizo Taquitos

makes 12 pieces **prep time** 15 minutes
cooking time 25 minutes

My girlfriends threw the most beautiful party for me and decided to prepare all Semi-Homemade® recipes that appear in this book. These taquitos were an absolute hit (as was the Black Bean Quesadilla, page 42). Both disappeared from their serving platters instantly. You're sure to get the same results when you serve them.

1   package (16-ounce, bulk) beef chorizo sausage, casing removed
1   cup medium chunky salsa, drained, *Pace*®
1   cup shredded mild cheddar cheese, *Kraft*®
6   fajita-size (8-inch) flour tortillas, *Mission*®
1   cup prepared guacamole (refrigerated section)
¼   cup sour cream

1. Preheat oven to 400 degrees F. In a large skillet, saute sausage over medium heat until brown, about 6 minutes. Drain fat from cooked sausage; discard. Set sausage aside to cool. Stir salsa and cheese into sausage in skillet.

2. Place 1 tortilla onto a clean work surface. Spoon ¼ cup of the sausage mixture down tortilla center. Fold tortilla in half, then roll up. Secure with toothpicks. Place on a foil-covered cookie sheet. Repeat with remaining tortillas and filling.

3. Bake until filling is hot and tortilla is crisp and golden brown, about 18 minutes. Cut taquitos in half crosswise. Serve hot with guacamole and sour cream.

Crabmeat Cucumber Rounds

makes 16 rounds **prep time** 15 minutes
cooling time 30 minutes

A little exotic and very tasty, these crab-topped cucumber rounds are a refreshing change in bite-size food. Remember to wash and dry the cucumber before slicing it, and please don't peel the skin. Before slicing you may want to use a fork to etch decorative lines down the side of the cucumber. This appetizer looks and tastes quite professional.

$1/4$ cup mayonnaise, *Best Foods® or Hellmann's®*
1 teaspoon prepared horseradish, *Morehouse®*
$1/2$ teaspoon Dijon mustard, *French's®*
$1/2$ teaspoon Worcestershire sauce, *Lea & Perrins®*
1 can (4.25-ounce) crabmeat, drained, *Geisha®*
$1/2$ large unpeeled English hothouse cucumber,
    cut crosswise into 16 thin slices (about $1/4$-inch slices)
8 pimiento-stuffed green olives, sliced, *Star®*

1. In a small bowl, mix together mayonnaise, horseradish, mustard, and Worcestershire sauce. Stir in crabmeat (be sure to drain all liquid from canned crabmeat). Cover and refrigerate for 30 minutes.

2. Arrange cucumber slices in a single layer on a serving tray. Spoon 1 tablespoon of crabmeat mixture onto each cucumber slice. Garnish with olive slices and serve.

Feta-Stuffed Artichoke Bottoms

makes about 15 pieces **prep time** 5 minutes **cooking time** 7 minutes

I have always loved to eat artichokes. When I was a child, my grandma would serve my sister Cynthia and me a whole artichoke to share. We would always argue about who would get to eat the "heart," as we called it. Really it was the bottom; ultimately, grandma would always make us split it. Years later, grandma gifted Cindy and me with a tour of the Holy Lands where we got to visit the great island of Santorini. We reminisced about our artichoke wars, while stuffing ourselves with these great Greek appetizers.

$1/2$ **cup chopped jarred roasted red bell peppers,** *Progresso*®
$1/4$ **cup chopped ripe olives (black),** *Early California*®
$1/4$ **cup crumbled feta cheese**
1   **tablespoon olive oil,** *Bertolli*®
1   **can ($13^3/4$-ounce) artichoke bottoms (approximately 15 pieces), drained and patted dry,** *Progresso*®

1. Preheat broiler. Line a cookie sheet with foil.

2. In a medium bowl, combine peppers, olives, cheese, and olive oil. Place artichoke bottoms onto prepared cookie sheet. Mound $1^1/2$ teaspoons of stuffing on each artichoke.

3. Broil 7 minutes or until golden on top. Transfer artichokes to a platter and serve hot.

Storage and Leftovers: Cover tightly and store in refrigerator for up to 1 day.

Oriental
Pork Purses

makes 24 purses **prep time** 15 minutes
cooking time 25 minutes

1	package (12-ounce) pork sausage, *Jimmy Dean*®
2	green onions, minced
1	tablespoon soy sauce, *Kikkoman*®
1	tablespoon hoisin sauce, *Sun Luck*®
$1/2$	teaspoon bottled minced garlic, *McCormick*®
24	square wonton wrappers, *Dynasty*®
	Nonstick vegetable cooking spray, *PAM*®
	Dipping sauces: purchased soy sauce, hoisin sauce, chili garlic sauce, and hot Chinese-style mustard

1. In a medium bowl, mix sausage, green onions, soy sauce, hoisin sauce, and garlic. Lay out 8 wonton wrappers on a clean surface and brush edges with water. Place about 1 tablespoon of pork mixture into center of each wrapper. Gather edges of wrapper together over filling. Press edges of wrapper together, enclosing filling completely. Repeat with remaining wrappers and filling.

2. Place a collapsible metal steamer rack in a large wide pot. Fill pot with $1/2$ inch of water. Spray steamer rack with nonstick spray. Bring water to a simmer. Working in batches, arrange purses on rack 1 inch apart.

3. Cover pot with lid and steam purses until cooked thoroughly, about 8 minutes. Watch the water level and add more water as needed. Transfer purses to platter. Serve with dipping sauces.

Smoked Salmon-and-Olive Blini

makes 32 blini **prep time** 15 minutes
cooking time 10 minutes

1	cup buckwheat pancake and waffle mix, *Aunt Jemima*®
1	cup whole milk
1	egg
1	tablespoon vegetable oil, *Wesson*®
	Nonstick vegetable cooking spray, *PAM*®
6	ounces sliced smoked salmon or lox, *Vita*®
3/4	cup kalamata olive spread, *Peloponnese*®
3/4	cup light sour cream
	Fresh dill, chopped
	Chopped ripe olives (black), *Early California*®

1. In a medium bowl, stir pancake mix, milk, egg, and oil until just blended. Set aside.

2. Spray griddle with nonstick cooking spray. Heat griddle over medium-low heat.

3. Spoon several 1-tablespoon dollops of batter onto griddle. Cook for 2 minutes or until bubbles appear, then turn blini over and cook for 1 minute. Set aside.

4. Cut salmon into 32 equal pieces. Place blini onto a platter. Spread each blini with 1 teaspoon of the olive spread. Top with a piece of smoked salmon, then with 1 teaspoon sour cream. Sprinkle with dill and chopped black olives.

Italian Fondue

servings 6 **prep time** 5 minutes
cooking time 10 minutes

I love to make this fondue and serve it in individual cups or bowls for each person. When entertaining, serve alongside crusty dinner rolls for an extra special touch. They're adorable, delicious, unique, and your guests will be amazed at your creative attention to detail.

2	tablespoons butter
2	tablespoons finely chopped fresh sage
2	tablespoons all-purpose flour, *Pillsbury*®
1¼	cups dry white wine, *Vendage*®
1	jar (16-ounce) Alfredo sauce, *Classico*®
1	package (8-ounce) shredded Six-Cheese Italian Blend (mozzarella, smoked provolone, Parmesan, Romano, fontina, and Asiago cheeses), *Sargento*®
	Dippers: crusty Italian bread, cubed; quartered figs; and cooked, cubed potatoes

1. Melt butter in a large heavy saucepan over medium heat. Add sage and cook until butter is golden brown, about 2 minutes.

2. Whisk in flour and cook for 1 minute. Whisk in wine and simmer for 2 minutes. Whisk in Alfredo sauce. Gradually add cheese, whisking until cheese melts and mixture is smooth.

3. Transfer mixture to a fondue pot, chafing dish, or ceramic bowl. Serve with dippers.

Fiesta Fondue

servings 6 **prep time** 5 minutes
cooking time 10 minutes

For sure, fondue is back! There are so many restaurants whose entire menus consist of different kinds of fondue. Hard to imagine there's such a demand that fondue alone could keep a place in business, but there is—which is why I've included such a wide variety of fondue options. Simple to make, this dish always earns glowing reviews.

1   can (10³/₄-ounce) cheddar cheese soup, *Campbell's*®
1   package (8-ounce) shredded sharp cheddar cheese, *Kraft*®
1   cup chunky chipotle salsa, *Pace*®
1   cup whole milk
     Dippers: French bread, cubed; jicama sticks; corn tortilla chips; and warm flour tortillas

1. Stir all ingredients, except dippers, in a medium heavy saucepan over medium heat until shredded cheese melts and mixture is smooth.

2. Transfer mixture to a fondue pot, chafing dish, or ceramic bowl. Serve with dippers.

White Chocolate
Fondue

servings 6 **prep time** 3 minutes
cooking time 7 minutes

White-chocolate-covered strawberries—people pay a fortune for these delicacies, but you can create the same specialties, if not better, with this sure-fire recipe. But don't stop with dipping strawberries. Ten years ago, I found *Ruffles*® ridged potato chips to be wonderful dipped in chocolate: the salt and chocolate are great together. Recently, high-end gourmet stores and catalogues began selling chocolate-covered potato chips for a small fortune. I should have cashed in on these chips myself! What's your favorite food to dip in chocolate? (See page 240.)

1   cup heavy cream
¹/₂   stick unsalted butter
2   packages (12 ounces each) premier white morsels, *Nestlé*®
      Dippers: sliced apples, bananas, strawberries, crisp cookies,
      pretzels, and cubed pound cake, *Sara Lee*®

1. In a large saucepan over medium heat, combine cream and butter. Bring mixture to a simmer, stirring constantly. Remove pan from heat.

2. Add white morsels. Stir until melted and smooth. Cool slightly.

3. Transfer to a fondue pot, chafing dish, or ceramic bowl. Serve with apples, bananas, strawberries, cookies, pretzels, and pound cake.

Dark Chocolate
Fondue

servings 6 **prep time** 3 minutes
cooking time 7 minutes

Quite honestly, you can eat this fondue with a spoon! Rich and decadent, it's on the same level as running your finger over a freshly frosted chocolate cake and placing that finger full of icing directly into your mouth. Heaven.

1   **cup heavy cream**
$^1/_2$ **stick unsalted butter**
1   **package (12-ounce) semisweet chocolate morsels,** *Hershey's*®
1   **package (12-ounce) milk chocolate morsels,** *Hershey's*®
    Dippers: sliced apples, bananas, strawberries, crisp cookies, pretzels, and cubed pound cake, *Sara Lee*®

1. In a large saucepan over medium heat, combine cream and butter. Bring mixture just to a simmer, stirring constantly. Remove pan from heat.

2. Add semisweet and milk chocolate morsels. Stir until melted and smooth. Cool slightly.

3. Transfer to a fondue pot, chafing dish, or ceramic bowl. Serve with apples, bananas, strawberries, cookies, pretzels, and pound cake.

Beer Margaritas

servings 4
prep time 2 minutes

Arriba, arriba! These Beer Margaritas will disappear in no time. You may as well double the recipe because everyone will want seconds.

1   lime, cut into 8 wedges
¼   cup coarse salt
2   bottles (12 ounces each) *Corona*® or your favorite beer, chilled
½   cup frozen concentrate limeade, thawed, *Minute Maid*®
½   cup chilled tequila, *Jose Cuervo Especial*®
     Ice cubes

1. Rub lime wedges around rims of 4 margarita glasses. Dip rims into salt to coat lightly.

2. In a medium pitcher, combine beer, limeade, and tequila. Fill prepared glasses with ice, then with margarita mixture.

3. Garnish with remaining lime wedges. Serve immediately.

Raspberry Sake

servings 6
prep time 5 minutes

A hot new sushi place opened up down the street from my office. While waiting there for a friend one evening, I had a quick drink—infused sake. Wow—how wonderful! Everyone around me was raving about it, and now so am I. The infusion method is difficult and time-consuming, so here's my shortcut to achieving a similar fabulous flavor.

1   bottle (750-ml) sake, chilled, *Gekkeikan*®
1   pint (16-ounce) canned wild berry juice cocktail concentrate, chilled, *Welch's*®
1   cup crushed ice
$\frac{1}{2}$ cup frozen raspberries, thawed
$\frac{1}{4}$ cup fresh lemon juice, or *ReaLemon*®

1. In a blender, combine sake, wild berry juice, ice, raspberries, and lemon juice. Pulse several times until raspberries are completely crushed.

2. Strain into 6 martini glasses. Serve immediately.

Gin Plush

servings 1 **prep time** 5 minutes

- 4 ice cubes
- 1/3 cup gin, *Tanqueray®*
- 1/4 cup guava nectar, *Kern's®*
- 1/4 cup pineapple juice, *Dole®*
- 1/4 cup orange juice, *Minute Maid®*
- 1/4 cup club soda, chilled, *Canada Dry®*

1. Place ice cubes and all ingredients in a large cocktail glass. Stir. Serve immediately.

Champagne Punch

servings 6 **prep time** 5 minutes **cooling time** 30 minutes

- 1 can (20-ounce) crushed pineapple in heavy syrup, *Dole®*
- 1 cup fresh lemon juice, or *ReaLemon®*
- 1 cup maraschino cherry juice, *Red Star®*
- 1 cup dark rum, *Myers's®*
- 1/2 cup brandy, *Christian Brothers®*
- 1 bottle (750-ml) chilled brut champagne, *Korbel®*

1. In a large punch bowl or pitcher, stir pineapple, lemon juice, cherry juice, rum, and brandy to blend. Refrigerate for 30 minutes. Add champagne just before serving.

Sour Apple Martini

servings 1 **prep time** 5 minutes

- 4 ice cubes
- 3 tablespoons apple sourball mix, *Hiram Walker®*
- 3 tablespoons vodka, *Smirnoff®*
- 2 teaspoons sweet vermouth
- 1 apple slice

1. In a cocktail shaker, combine all ingredients except the apple slice. Cover and shake for 15 seconds. Strain into a martini glass and garnish with the apple slice. Serve immediately.

Cubana Rum

servings 1 **prep time** 5 minutes

- 1/3 cup apricot nectar, *Kern's®*
- 1/4 cup fresh lime juice, or sweetened lime juice, *Rose's®*
- 1/4 cup apricot brandy, *Hiram Walker®*
- 1/4 cup light rum, *Bacardi®*
- 4 ice cubes

1. Combine all ingredients in a cocktail shaker. Cover and shake for 15 seconds. Strain into a glass and serve immediately.

Clockwise from lower right:
Gin Plush, Champagne Punch,
Cubana Rum, Sour Apple Martini

Sassy Sangría

servings 8 **prep time** 8 minutes
cooling time 3 hours

Great for a brunch or just a bunch, this Sassy Sangría carries a powerful punch—careful or you'll be singing the latest Gypsy Kings CD yourself.

3	cups chianti, *Villa Antinori*®
1	cup brandy, *Christian Brothers*®
¼	cup triple sec, *Hiram Walker*®
1	orange, sliced
1	lime, sliced
1	lemon, sliced
1	apple, cored and diced
8	fresh raspberries
2	cups club soda, chilled, *Schweppes*®

1. In a large pitcher, combine all ingredients except club soda. Cover tightly and refrigerate 3 hours.

2. Pour ¾ cup sangria mixture and ¼ cup club soda into each glass, dividing fruit equally. Serve immediately.

Berry Smooth

servings 4 **prep time** 3 minutes

2   cups chilled lemonade, *Minute Maid*®
1/2 cup cassis liqueur, *Hiram Walker*®, or
     blackberry brandy, *Hiram Walker*®
1/2 cup vodka, *Smirnoff*®
2   tablespoons lime juice, or sweetened
     lime juice, *Rose's*®
2   cups ice cubes

1. In a pitcher, stir all ingredients, except ice. Fill glasses with ice, then with equal portions lemonade mixture. Serve immediately.

Cool Red Wine

servings 6 **prep time** 5 minutes **cooling time** 1 hour

1   bottle (750-ml) Beaujolais, chilled, *Louis Jadot*®
1   can (15-ounce) sliced peaches in heavy syrup,
     Del Monte®
1   orange, sliced
1/2 cup orange liqueur, *Cointreau*®
1/2 cup orange juice, *Minute Maid*®
1/4 cup granulated sugar, *C&H*®

1. Stir all ingredients in a large pitcher. Cover tightly and refrigerate for 1 hour. Fill glasses with equal portions of red wine mixture. Serve immediately.

Sherry Fruit Bowl

servings 6 **prep time** 5 minutes **cooling time** 1 hour

1   container (16-ounce) frozen sweetened
     sliced strawberries, thawed
1   can (15-ounce) sliced peaches (with juice), *S&W*®
1   cup dry sherry or Madeira, *Paul Masson*®
1   bottle (750-ml) chilled Chardonnay, *Vendage*®

1. In a punch bowl or pitcher, stir strawberries (with syrup), peaches (with juice), and sherry or Madeira. Refrigerate for 1 hour. Stir in wine and serve immediately.

Scarlet O'Brandy

servings 1 **prep time** 2 minutes

1   cup crushed ice
1/3 cup whiskey, *Southern Comfort*®
1/3 cup cranberry juice cocktail, *Ocean Spray*®
2   tablespoons fresh lime juice, or sweetened lime juice,
     Rose's®
1   orange wedge

1. Combine all ingredients, except orange wedge, in cocktail shaker. Cover and shake for 15 seconds. Strain into glass and garnish with orange wedge. Serve immediately.

Clockwise from lower right:
Berry Smooth, Sherry Fruit Bowl, Cool Red
Wine, Scarlet O'Brandy

Soups and Salads

Served as a snack, light lunch, side dish, or main meal, soups and salads are always welcome.
The savviest of chefs know that soups and salads as stand-alones or as starters to a main course
are foolproof ways to ensure a successful meal. Who doesn't love to have a fresh, crisp salad?
Or a steaming bowl of flavorful soup? Both are staples of any diet.

Soups and salads are a tasty and easy way to meet your daily requirements of nutrients and vitamins.
They're also among the quickest courses to create. Those of us who are watching our diets can look
forward to soups and salads as satisfying, low-calorie feasts.

By adding the smallest accoutrements, you can change the flavor, texture, and presentation of
your soups or salads. Garnishes as simple as toasted almonds, sweet candied walnuts, a dollop
of cumin-flavored sour cream, or a decorative piece of puff pastry are easy to add and a great way
to show off your culinary creativity.

The Recipes

Crabby Bisque

servings 2 **prep time** 5 minutes
cooking time 6 minutes

This is a soup among soups. Not much compares to this flavorful Crabby Bisque. This "must make" is super to serve in coffee mugs and makes the most unique appetizer sipper.

1   can (10½-ounce) restaurant-style condensed crab bisque,
        Bookbinder's®
¾   cup plus 2 tablespoons heavy cream
1   tablespoon chopped fresh parsley
1   can (4.25-ounce) crabmeat, *Geisha*®
1   tablespoon fresh lemon juice, or *ReaLemon*®
     Salt and cayenne pepper

1. In a medium saucepan, combine bisque, ¾ cup of the heavy cream, and parsley. Bring to a boil. Stir in crabmeat with juices. Bring to a simmer. Add lemon juice. Season to taste with salt and cayenne pepper.

2. Spoon soup into 2 bowls. Divide the remaining 2 tablespoons cream between the bowls, swirl with butter knife to create design, and serve.

Storage and Leftovers: Cover tightly and store in refrigerator for up to 1 day. Reheat in a saucepan over low heat, stirring frequently until warm.

Roasted Pepper Soup

servings 2 **prep time** 3 minutes
cooking time 5 minutes

When a friend of mine told me of his family's traditional Roasted Pepper Soup, it didn't sound particularly appetizing to me. Once I tasted it, I begged him to allow me to share the recipe with you. This is an amazing combination of flavors that work incredibly well together and can only enhance any meal it accompanies.

1	can (14-ounce) chicken broth, *Swanson*®
1	cup jarred roasted bell peppers, rinsed and drained, *Progresso*®
¾	cup orange juice, *Minute Maid*®
¼	cup dry sherry, *Christian Brothers*®
2	tablespoons red wine vinegar, *Heinz*®
2	garlic cloves
	Salt and pepper
	Light sour cream

1. In a blender, combine broth, roasted peppers, orange juice, sherry, vinegar, and garlic. Pulse until smooth.

2. Transfer soup to a medium saucepan and bring to a slow boil, stirring occasionally. Season to taste with salt and pepper.

3. Ladle soup into two bowls. Spoon a dollop of sour cream on top of soup and serve.

Storage and Leftovers: Cover tightly and store in refrigerator for up to 2 days. Reheat in a saucepan over low heat, stirring frequently until warm.

Golden Mushroom Soup

servings 2 **prep time** 5 minutes
cooking time 10 minutes

When my girlfriend Barbara describes something she thinks is amazing, she says it's "beyond." Barbara would say, this soup is "beyond." It's that good. So double the recipe to be sure there's enough to go around a second time—you'll need it.

- 2 tablespoons olive oil, *Bertolli*®
- 1 large, fresh portobello mushroom, gills scraped off and mushroom finely chopped
- 1 can (10¾-ounce) condensed golden mushroom soup, *Campbell's*®
- 1 cup water
- ¾ cup heavy cream
- 1 teaspoon bottled minced garlic, *McCormick*®

1. In a large saucepan over medium-high heat, warm olive oil. Saute mushroom until tender, about 2 minutes.

2. Mix in soup, water, cream, and garlic. Bring soup to a simmer, stirring occasionally, about 5 minutes.

3. Ladle soup into 2 bowls and serve.

Note: Garnish with a slice of white mushroom and an herb of your choice, such as thyme.

Storage and Leftovers: Cover tightly and store in refrigerator for up to 3 days. Reheat in a saucepan over low heat, stirring frequently until warm.

Sante Fe Five-Bean Soup

servings 8 **prep time** 8 minutes
cooking time 10 minutes

1	can (15-ounce) black beans, drained, *S&W*®
1	can (15-ounce) kidney beans, drained, *S&W*®
1	can (15-ounce) garbanzo beans, drained, *S&W*®
1	can (15-ounce) red beans, drained, *S&W*®
1	can (15-ounce) navy (or white) beans, drained, *S&W*®
1	can (14½-ounce) chopped tomatoes, *Del Monte*®
1	can (14-ounce) chicken broth, *Swanson*®
¾	cup chunky salsa, *Pace*®
2	teaspoons ground cumin, *McCormick*®
1	teaspoon dried red pepper flakes, *McCormick*®
½	cup light sour cream
1	cup chopped onions

1. Puree black beans in a blender.

2. In a large pot, stir all the remaining beans, the tomatoes, broth, salsa, cumin, and red pepper flakes. Stir in pureed black beans. Cover and simmer for 10 minutes, stirring occasionally, until hot.

3. Ladle soup into bowls. Garnish with sour cream and onions. Serve hot.

Note: For a smoother texture, entire soup can be pureed. Pureed soup can be chilled and used as a dip for chips, vegetables, or for a sauce to serve with rice.

Storage and Leftovers: Cover tightly and store in refrigerator for up to 3 days. Reheat in a saucepan over medium heat, stirring frequently until warm.

Creamy Curried Carrot Soup

servings 6 **prep time** 10 minutes
cooking time 18 minutes

1 tablespoon vegetable oil, *Wesson*®
2 packages (8 ounces each) shredded carrots,
　　rinsed and drained, *Ready Pac*®
1 small onion, chopped
2 teaspoons bottled minced garlic, *McCormick*®
1 tablespoon curry powder, *McCormick*®
1 can (14-ounce) chicken broth, *Swanson*®
2/3 cup whole milk
2/3 cup heavy cream
　 Salt and pepper
　 Plain yogurt, *Dannon*®
　 Fresh cilantro, chopped

1. Heat oil in a heavy large pot over medium heat. Add carrots, onion, garlic, and curry powder. Saute until onion is tender, about 2 minutes.

2. Add broth, milk, and cream. Simmer until carrots are tender, stirring occasionally, about 15 minutes.

3. Working in batches, puree carrot mixture in a blender until smooth. Return soup to pot. Season to taste with salt and pepper.

4. Ladle soup into bowls. Garnish with yogurt and cilantro. Serve hot.

Note: Soup also can be chilled and served cold.

Storage and Leftovers: Cover tightly and store in refrigerator for up to 3 days. Reheat in a saucepan over low heat, stirring frequently until warm.

Bay Shrimp and Avocado Salad

servings 2
prep time 5 minutes

Avocados are the best—but have you ever tried to grow an avocado tree with a pit, a couple of toothpicks, and a shallow dish of water? Impossible! Whoever thought this one up is still getting a good laugh. But laughs will not be what you get when you serve this sensational salad.

When picking out avocados, be sure to choose firm fruits—not rock hard ones—that give a little under gentle pressure.

For easy seeding, use a sharp knife to cut the avocado lengthwise through the flesh to the seed.

Separate the halves by placing one hand on each side of the avocado and twisting in opposite directions.

To remove the seed, tap it with the blade of a sharp knife. When the blade catches in the seed, rotate the knife to lift out the seed.

8 ounces fresh bay shrimp
1 cup shredded carrots, rinsed and drained, *Ready Pac*®
½ cup frozen petite peas, thawed, *Green Giant*®
½ cup frozen cut corn kernels, thawed, *Green Giant*®
4 tablespoons Champagne vinaigrette, *Girard's*®
   Salt and pepper
1 firm, ripe avocado, halved and pitted

1. Toss shrimp, carrots, peas, corn, and 3 tablespoons of the vinaigrette in a medium bowl to coat.

2. Season shrimp salad to taste with salt and pepper.

3. Place one avocado half onto each of 2 plates. Divide shrimp salad on top of avocado halves. Drizzle remaining 1 tablespoon vinaigrette over avocado halves and serve.

Apple Slaw

servings 4 **prep time** 10 minutes
cooling time 20 minutes

Amazingly easy! Amazingly good! This Apple Slaw breathes new life into old coleslaw. It's tangy with a hint of sweetness. You'll want to share this recipe with everyone you know.

$3/4$ **cup sour cream**
$1/4$ **cup granulated sugar, *C&H*®**
3   **tablespoons apple cider vinegar, *Heinz*®**
2   **tablespoons dry ranch salad dressing mix, *Hidden Valley*®**
1   **package (8-ounce) shredded cabbage and carrots, *Ready Pac*®**
3   **green apples, cored and diced**
4   **green onions, thinly sliced**
    Salt and pepper

1. Whisk sour cream, sugar, vinegar, and ranch seasoning in a large bowl to blend.

2. Add cabbage mixture, apples, and green onions. Toss to coat.

3. Season to taste with salt and pepper. Cover tightly and chill 20 minutes or up to 4 hours. Serve cold.

Candied Walnut Butter Salad

servings 4 **prep time** 8 minutes
cooking time 12 minutes

Candied Walnuts

Nonstick vegetable cooking spray, *PAM*®
4 **tablespoons granulated sugar, *C&H*®**
1 **tablespoon orange-tangerine juice, *Minute Maid*®**
1 **cup walnut halves, *Diamond*®**
1/4 **teaspoon ground cinnamon, *McCormick*®**

Salad

2 **heads butter lettuce, washed and drained**
1 **can (8-ounce) mandarin orange segments, drained, *Del Monte*®**
1/4 **red onion, very thinly sliced**
1/2 **cup purchased Asian-style salad dressing (such as miso dressing or ginger dressing)**

Candied Walnuts Preparation

1. Preheat oven to 375 degrees F. Line a large cookie sheet with foil and spray with nonstick spray.

2. In a 10-inch skillet over medium heat, add 3 tablespoons of the sugar and the orange-tangerine juice. Bring to a simmer, then add walnuts. Cook until sugar is absorbed and mixture starts to caramelize around walnuts, stirring constantly, about 2 minutes.

3. In a small bowl, mix cinnamon and remaining 1 tablespoon sugar. Toss walnuts in cinnamon-sugar mixture. Place walnuts in single layer on prepared cookie sheet. Bake until walnuts appear crystallized and toasted, about 8 minutes. Set aside.

Salad Preparation

4. Arrange 4 to 6 lettuce leaves on each plate. Randomly place orange segments, onion slices, and walnuts on top of each lettuce bed. Drizzle 2 tablespoons of dressing on top of each salad and serve.

Spicy Crab Salad

servings 2 **prep time** 10 minutes
cooling time 15 minutes

This salad is a meal in itself. As good as it looks, it tastes even better. It can be made ahead and easily stored for serving later. If there's any extra, don't throw it out—this salad is a scrumptious leftover (even if there are only a few bites left).

3   tablespoons mayonnaise, *Best Foods®* or *Hellmann's®*
1   tablespoon fresh lemon juice, or *ReaLemon®*
1   tablespoon seafood seasoning, *Chef Paul Prudhomme's Seafood Magic Seasoning Blend®*
1   tablespoon red wine vinegar, *Heinz®*
1   cup cooked white rice ($1/4$ cup uncooked rice), *Minute® Rice*
1   can (4.25-ounce) crabmeat, *Geisha®*
3   tablespoons sliced ripe olives (black), *Early California®*
4   small green olives, sliced, *Star®*
1   small tomato, diced
10 thin asparagus spears, trimmed and cut into $1/2$-inch pieces (lightly steamed, if desired)
    Salt and pepper
    Fresh basil leaves (optional)

1. In a large bowl, whisk mayonnaise, lemon juice, seafood seasoning, and vinegar to blend. Add rice, crabmeat, and olives. Toss gently to blend. Fold in tomato and asparagus.

2. Cover and refrigerate for 15 minutes. Season to taste with salt and pepper before serving. Garnish with fresh basil leaves (optional).

Restaurant Remakes

It all started with Cinnabons®. I went to the mall and watched while the baker whipped up a batch in the window, then baked them to heady perfection and smothered them in sweet icing. As I concocted their clone in my own kitchen, I wondered what other restaurant favorites I could remake the Semi-Homemade® way. Soon I was cooking up all sorts of guilty pleasures—Coney Island chili dogs, soft pretzels, orange smoothies, and iced brownie cappuccinos, every bite as blissful as the ones found at the mall.

Mall food is fun food. A mere whiff brings mouthwatering anticipation; a bite, a piece of heaven. From melt-in-your-mouth sweets to take-out dinners to fast breakfast breaks and chic coffeehouse creations, these made-at-home remakes treat you to a quick fix without ever leaving the house.

The Recipes

Cinnamon Buns

makes 16 rolls **prep time** 30 minutes
rising time 1 hour **baking time** 15 minutes

A Food Network website favorite. When it comes to naughty food, Cinnabons® take the cake. My recipe is a ringer for the original, from the sugar-cinnamon dough to the deliciously drippy cream cheese icing. Make baby ones for a quick mini munchie or jumbo ones to share shamelessly, but be sure to get the center—it's the best part!

Dough and Filling
1   loaf frozen white bread dough, thawed*, *Bridgford*®
     All-purpose flour, for dusting surface
1   cup packed golden brown sugar, *C&H*®
1   tablespoon ground cinnamon, *McCormick*®
$2/3$ stick butter, softened

Icing
1   stick unsalted butter, softened
1   cup powdered sugar, *C&H*®
$1/3$ cup cream cheese, *Philadelphia*®
1   teaspoon vanilla extract, *McCormick*®

Dough and Filling Preparation
1. Roll out dough onto a lightly floured surface to form a 15×7-inch rectangle. In a small bowl, combine brown sugar and cinnamon; set aside. Spread $2/3$ stick softened butter over dough. Sprinkle evenly with cinnamon–sugar mixture. Starting at the long edge, roll up dough as for a jelly roll. Pinch seam to seal.

2. Cut rolled dough into 16 slices and divide slices between 2 lightly buttered 8-inch round baking pans. Set aside in a warm place and allow dough to rise until doubled in size, about 1 hour.

3. Preheat oven to 400 degrees F. Bake for 15 minutes or until golden on top. Promptly invert baking pan over a wire rack, and lift pan from buns. Scoop filling that has remained in the pan over buns. Allow buns to cool slightly, about 10 minutes.

Icing Preparation
4. Meanwhile, beat the icing ingredients with an electric mixer until fluffy. Spread or pipe (with a pastry bag) icing over rolls. Serve warm.

***Note:** Thaw frozen bread dough overnight in the refrigerator.

Soft Pretzels

makes 14 pretzels **prep time** 20 minutes
cooking time 30 minutes

In Latin, *pretzel* means "a little reward"—fitting because every time I go to the mall, I reward myself with one of these tasty little treats. Pretzels are the perfect "mood food," seasoned sweet, savory, or spicy to suit your mood. To make them pillowy soft, boil them in water first, then bake.

1　loaf frozen white bread dough, thawed*, *Bridgford*®
　All-purpose flour, for dusting surface, *Pillsbury*®
1　egg, lightly beaten
1/2　cup coarse salt (optional)

1. Line a sheet pan with waxed paper. Divide dough into 14 pieces. On a lightly floured surface, roll each piece of dough into a 16-inch rope and form into a pretzel shape. Transfer dough to prepared sheet pan; cover and refrigerate until ready to boil.

2. Preheat oven to 400 degrees F. Lightly butter a sheet pan. In a large pot, bring 4 quarts of water to a boil. Add pretzels, 3 at a time, and cook until pretzels rise to the surface, about 2 minutes. Remove and drain on paper towels.

3. Arrange pretzels 3 inches apart on prepared sheet pan. Brush with beaten egg. Sprinkle with coarse salt or with choice of toppings. Bake for 15 to 20 minutes or until brown.

***Note:** Thaw frozen bread dough overnight in the refrigerator.

Garlic Cheese Pretzels

1/2　cup finely grated Parmesan, *Kraft*®
1　teaspoon garlic powder, *McCormick*®

1. After pretzels are poached and just before baking, brush pretzels with beaten egg (as directed above). Sprinkle with Parmesan and garlic powder. Bake for 15 to 20 minutes or until brown.

Cinnamon Pretzels

1/2　cup powdered sugar, *C&H*®
1　tablespoon ground cinnamon, *McCormick*®
1/4　cup honey, *Sue Bee*®

1. In a small bowl, combine powdered sugar and cinnamon with 1 to 2 tablespoons water (enough water to make a glaze); set aside. After pretzels are poached and just before baking (as directed above), brush pretzels with honey instead of beaten egg. Bake for 15 to 20 minutes, or until brown. Remove pretzels from oven. While still warm, brush with cinnamon-sugar glaze.

Coney Island Chili Dogs

servings 8 **prep time** 15 minutes
cooking time 25 minutes

In college, my best friend Colleen and I would hop in the car to get chili dogs or corn dogs and root beer floats at least three nights a week. My version delivers the same fun on the run but uses higher quality ingredients, like lean ground beef. (You can always substitute ground turkey or ground chicken, if desired, to be even more healthful.) The secret ingredient, however, is yellow mustard—its old-fashioned kick makes the years melt away.

1   pound ground beef, 85% lean
1   bottle (12-ounce) chili sauce, *Heinz®*
1   packet (1.48-ounce) chili seasoning, *Lawry's®*
½   cup water
1   teaspoon Worcestershire sauce, *Lea & Perrins®*
1   tablespoon yellow mustard, *French's®*
½   teaspoon onion powder, *McCormick®*
8   beef hot dogs
8   hot dog buns
      Shredded cheddar cheese, *Kraft®*
      Chopped white onion

1. In a large pot over medium heat, brown ground beef. Add chili sauce, chili seasoning, water, Worcestershire sauce, mustard, and onion powder. Bring to boil. Lower heat and simmer for 30 minutes.

2. Meanwhile, cook hot dogs according to package instructions.

3. Place hot dogs in buns; top with chili, cheddar cheese, and chopped onion.

Orange Smoothie

servings 2
prep time 5 minutes

1   can (16-ounce) frozen orange juice concentrate
1   packet (1-ounce) sugar-free, fat-free vanilla pudding mix, *Jell-O®*
1   container (4-ounce) orange cream yogurt, *Yoplait®*
1   cup low-fat milk
3   cups ice cubes

1. Combine orange juice concentrate, pudding mix, yogurt, milk, and ice cubes in a blender. Cover and blend until smooth. Divide between 2 glasses.

Beef and Vegetable Stir-Fry

servings 6 **prep time** 15 minutes
cooking time 15 minutes

2 tablespoons vegetable oil, *Wesson®*
½ pound boneless top sirloin steak, thinly sliced
½ cup onion, sliced into strips
1 tablespoon bottled minced garlic, *McCormick®*
1 tablespoon minced ginger
1 bag (12-ounce) fresh vegetable stir-fry mix
1 package (6-ounce) frozen sliced mushrooms, *PictSweet®*
1 can (8-ounce) sliced water chestnuts, *Geisha®*
1 red bell pepper, sliced into strips
2 tablespoons oyster sauce, *Dynasty®*
1 packet (1-ounce) stir-fry seasoning mix, *Kikkoman®*
    (dissolved in 2 tablespoons of water)
½ teaspoon red pepper flakes

1. In a large skillet or wok, heat 1 tablespoon of the oil over high heat. Add beef and stir-fry for 3 minutes. Remove from pan.

2. Add the remaining 1 tablespoon oil to pan and saute onion, garlic, and ginger. Add mixed vegetables and stir-fry for 3 minutes. Add mushrooms, water chestnuts, and red bell pepper. Stir-fry for another 3 minutes. Return beef to pan and stir in oyster sauce, seasoning mix, and pepper flakes; stir-fry for 3 more minutes. Serve with steamed rice.

White-Chocolate Dipped Fortune Cookies

makes 12 cookies **prep time** 20 minutes
cooling time 20 minutes

½ cup white dipping chocolate, *Baker's®*
½ cup semisweet chocolate morsels, *Nestlé®*
12 fortune cookies
    Decorating sugar

1. Line a baking sheet with waxed paper or plastic wrap. Melt the two chocolates in separate small bowls. Dip the fortune cookies in either the white or semisweet chocolate, covering half or whole cookie. Sprinkle with decorating sugar. Place onto baking sheet to cool.

Onion Blooms

makes 4 blooms **prep time** 15 minutes
cooking time 10 to 12 minutes

They're called many things—onion loaves, awesome blossoms, Texas tumbleweeds—and I crave them all the time. They're gorgeous, dramatic, positively perfect, but not at all difficult to make. The trick is to add club soda to the batter. It makes the crust light, fluffy, and irresistibly crunchy—just the right contrast to my zesty dipping sauce.

	Vegetable oil, *Wesson*®
3	cups all-purpose flour, *Pillsbury*®
2	packets (1 ounce each) dry ranch salad dressing mix, *Hidden Valley*®
4	large Vidalia onions
2	boxes tempura (8 ounces each) batter mix, *McCormick*® *Golden Dipt*®
2	cups club soda, chilled, *Schweppes*®

1. Fill fryer with vegetable oil to its maximum level*. Preheat oil to 375 degrees F.

2. Combine flour and ranch dressing mix in a shallow bowl. Set aside. Cut about 1/2 inch off the onion tops and peel them. Cut 12 vertical slices to just above the bottom of onion. Do not cut all the way through the onion. Remove center of each onion and save for other recipes.

3. Mix tempura batter with chilled club soda. Batter should be slightly lumpy. Cover each onion in seasoned flour, shaking to remove excess flour. Dip into tempura batter, spreading "petals" to coat onion evenly with batter.

4. Carefully place 1 onion into fryer. Fry about 2 to 3 minutes or until golden. Remove and drain on paper towels. Repeat with remaining onions. Serve hot with Spicy Mayo Dip.

*Note: If you don't have a fryer, you can use a large stockpot. Select a pot that's twice as big as the onion and clip a deep-fat-frying thermometer to the side to monitor the temperature. Pour in enough canola oil to completely cover the onion. **Never leave the pot unattended because the oil can catch on fire.**

Spicy Mayo Dip

makes about 2 1/4 cups
prep time 5 minutes

2	cups low-fat mayonnaise, *Best Foods*® or *Hellmann's*®
1	packet (1.5-ounce) sun-dried tomato pesto mix, *Knorr*®
4	tablespoons spicy ketchup, *Heinz*® *Ketchup Kick'rs*®

1. Mix all ingredients in a bowl. Serve with Onion Blooms.

Bacon, Egg, and Cheese Croissants

makes 4 sandwiches **prep time** 25 minutes
cooking time 30 minutes

8	slices bacon
1	can (8-ounce) crescent rolls, *Pillsbury®*
2	tablespoons butter, melted
3	tablespoons mayonnaise, *Hellmann's®* or *Best Foods®*
3	tablespoons sour cream
1	teaspoon dry ranch dressing mix, *Hidden Valley®*
1/2	teaspoon Dijon mustard
	Nonstick cooking spray, *PAM®*
4	eggs
4	slices American cheese, *Kraft®*

1. Preheat oven to 375 degrees F. Lay bacon slices onto a baking sheet. Bake for 30 minutes or until bacon is browned, rotating the pan halfway through cooking time. Drain on paper towels and set aside.

2. Meanwhile, unroll crescent dough. Separate the 4 rectangles. Starting with 1 rectangle, separate the triangles and pinch together the 2 shorter sides making 1 large triangle. Roll up the triangle starting from the longest side to form large crescent roll. Bring the ends around and overlap to form a bun. Place onto a baking sheet. Repeat with remaining 3 pieces. Brush rolls with melted butter. Bake for 11 to 13 minutes. To make sauce, combine mayo, sour cream, ranch dressing mix, and mustard. Set aside until ready to assemble sandwich.

3. To cook the eggs, spray the bottom of a nonstick skillet with cooking spray; heat pan over medium heat. With cooking spray, spray the inside of a clean dry ring mold (or a tuna can with the top and bottom removed). Heat mold in pan. Crack an egg into the mold and break the yolk. Season with salt and pepper. Place a small plate on top of the mold and cook egg for 3 to 4 minutes until set. Turn egg if top is not set. Remove to a plate and repeat with remaining eggs.

4. Split each roll horizontally and spread both halves with sauce. Place 1 egg on bottom half. Add a slice of cheese, 2 slices of bacon, and top of roll. Heat each sandwich in the microwave for 20 to 30 seconds until cheese starts to melt.

Cheesy Sausage English Muffins

makes 4 sandwiches **prep time** 10 minutes
cooking time 20 minutes

4	fresh sausage patties, *Farmer John®* or *Jimmy Dean®*
4	English muffins, split in half, *Thomas'®*
4	slices American cheese, *Kraft®*

1. Preheat oven to 375 degrees F. Flatten sausage patty to 1/4-inch thickness. Place patties on baking sheet. Bake for 20 minutes, turning patties once. Place on plate lined with paper towels; set aside.

2. Meanwhile, toast English muffins. Place a sausage patty on bottom half of each muffin. Add a slice of cheese and muffin top. Heat each sandwich in the microwave for 20 to 30 seconds until cheese starts to melt.

Iced Brownie Cappuccino

servings 2
prep time 10 minutes

2	shots espresso or $^1/_2$ cup very strong coffee
1	cup ice cubes
$^1/_2$	cup sweetened condensed milk
$^1/_2$	cup frozen whipped topping, thawed, *Cool Whip*®
2	tablespoons chocolate syrup, *Hershey's*®
3	tablespoons semisweet chocolate morsels, *Nestlé*®
	Frozen whipped topping, thawed, *Cool Whip*® (optional)
	Chocolate syrup, *Hershey's*® (optional)

1. Combine espresso, ice cubes, condensed milk, the $^1/_2$ cup whipped topping, the 2 tablespoons chocolate syrup, and the chocolate morsels. Blend until smooth. Divide between 2 glasses. If desired, put some whipped topping into a pastry bag fitted with a star tip or into a plastic resealable bag with a small hole cut in one corner. Pipe whipped topping on top of each drink and drizzle with chocolate syrup (optional).

Strawberry Nirvana Jamba

servings 2
prep time 10 minutes

1$^1/_2$	cups frozen strawberries
1	banana, peeled and cut in large chunks
1	cup strawberry-banana juice blend, *Langer's*®
3	tablespoons powdered nonfat dry milk
	Ice
	Whey protein powder (optional)
	Fresh strawberries, for garnish
	Banana slices, for garnish

1. Add strawberries, banana, strawberry-banana juice, powdered milk, ice, and whey protein (optional) to blender. Cover and blend on high speed until well blended. Add enough ice to make mixture of smoothie consistency. Divide between 2 glasses to serve. Top each drink with a fresh strawberry and banana slices.

Slow Cooker Meals

With a slow cooker, dinner cooks itself! I've always loved made-from-scratch meals, but my hectic schedule really eats into my cooking time. Then I rediscovered Grandma's favorite timesaver—the humble slow cooker. Just add your ingredients, turn it on when you leave in the morning, and dinner's ready when you come home at night.

This chapter is full of one-pot wonders—succulent chicken simmering in wine sauce, thick chowders, stew with vegetables, and marinated meatballs in zesty marinara, all prepped in minutes, leaving leftovers for lunch. Inexpensive cuts of meat cook up juicy and tender, their drippings make flavorful gravy, and the house smells heavenly when you walk in the door. Whether you're cooking for a crowd, a family, or just one, slow cooking is a fast, easy way to get a delicious dinner on the table.

The Recipes

Chicken with White Wine Sauce

servings 6 **prep time** 15 minutes
cooking time 8 hours (Low) or 3 to 4 hours (High)

This flavorful dish couldn't be simpler—or more elegant—at home on family night as it is when company comes. The secret is a subtle wine sauce that makes the chicken moist and juicy. The alcohol in the wine evaporates during cooking, leaving only the fabulous flavor that everyone fancies.

24 pearl onions, peeled
8   ounces mushrooms, sliced
4   strips thick-sliced bacon
4   pounds meaty chicken pieces
    Salt and pepper
1   can (10¾-ounce) cream of chicken soup, *Campbell's*®
1   cup dry white wine, *Vendage*®
2   teaspoons Italian seasoning, *McCormick*®
2   teaspoons bottled minced garlic, *McCormick*®

1. Add pearl onions and sliced mushrooms to a 4- to 5-quart slow cooker.

2. In a large skillet over medium heat, fry bacon until crispy. Reserve bacon for garnish. Discard all but 2 tablespoons of bacon fat. Season cut-up chicken with salt and pepper. Over medium-high heat, brown chicken pieces on all sides in bacon fat. Place browned chicken into slow cooker.

3. In a medium bowl, stir together cream of chicken soup, white wine, Italian seasoning, and garlic. Pour over chicken. Cover and cook on low-heat setting for 8 hours or high-heat setting for 3 to 4 hours.

4. If desired, remove skin from chicken. Ladle with white wine sauce and garnish with crumbled bacon.

Beef Pot Roast

servings 8 **prep time** 10 minutes
cooking time 8 to 9 hours (Low) or 3 to 4 hours (High)

1   bag (12-ounce) frozen onions
1   bag (8-ounce) frozen carrot slices
1   beef chuck roast (4-pound), rinsed and patted dry
    Salt and pepper
2   tablespoons vegetable oil, *Wesson*®
1   can (10¾-ounce) condensed cream of celery soup, *Campbell's*®
1   packet (1-ounce) onion soup mix, *Lipton*®
1   cup low-sodium beef broth, *Swanson*®
¼   cup steak sauce, *A1 Steak Sauce*®

1. Add frozen onions and carrots to the bottom of a 4- to 5-quart slow cooker.

2. Season roast with salt and pepper. Heat oil in a large skillet over medium-high heat. Brown chuck roast on all sides, then place into slow cooker on top of onions and carrots.

3. In a medium bowl, stir together cream of celery soup, onion soup mix, beef broth, and steak sauce. Pour over top of roast.

4. Cover slow cooker and cook on low-heat setting for 8 to 9 hours or high-heat setting for 3 to 4 hours.

Mediterranean Vegetable Stew

servings 8 **prep time** 10 minutes
cooking time 8 hours (Low) or 4 hours (High)

This savory stew is as soulfully satisfying as a trip to the Mediterranean. It's the perfect "Mommy Meal," a versatile dish that can be made in advance and refrigerated or frozen until time to serve. Ideal for lunch or dinner, warm as an entrée or cool as a companion to salad.

1 bag (8-ounce) Mediterranean-style frozen vegetable mix
2 zucchini, diced
1 red onion, diced
1 teaspoon bottled minced garlic, *McCormick*®
1 can (15.5-ounce) garbanzo beans, drained, *S&W*®
1 can (14.5-ounce) diced tomatoes with basil, garlic,
      and oregano, *Hunt's*®
1 can (14-ounce) low-sodium vegetable broth, *Swanson*®
1 can (10¾-ounce) condensed tomato soup, *Campbell's*®
1 packet (0.5-ounce) pesto mix, *Knorr*®
   Salt and pepper
   Fresh flat-leaf parsley (optional)

1. Add frozen vegetables, zucchini, red onion, garlic, garbanzo beans, tomatoes, broth, tomato soup, and pesto mix to a 4- to 5-quart slow cooker. Stir to combine.

2. Cover and cook on low-heat setting for 8 hours or high-heat setting for 4 hours. Season to taste with salt and pepper.

3. Ladle into bowls and garnish with flat-leaf parsley (optional). Serve with crusty French bread.

Chinese Braised Short Ribs

servings 8 **prep time** 15 minutes
cooking time 9 to 10 hours (Low) or 3 to 4 hours (High)

1	large onion, sliced
4	pounds beef short ribs
	Lemon pepper
	Garlic salt
2	tablespoons canola oil, *Wesson*®
2	cups low-sodium beef broth, *Swanson*®
1	packet (1.1-ounces) beefy onion soup mix, *Lipton*®
2	cans (14.5 ounces each) tomatoes with green pepper, celery, and onion, *Hunt's*®
2	tablespoons five-spice powder

1. Add sliced onion to the bottom of a 4- to 5-quart slow cooker. Season short ribs with lemon pepper and garlic salt. Heat oil in large skillet over medium-high heat. Working in batches, brown all sides of short ribs. Place into slow cooker on top of onion.

2. In a medium bowl, stir together remaining ingredients. Pour over the top of short ribs. Cover and cook on low-heat setting for 9 to 10 hours or high-heat setting for 3 to 4 hours.

Note: Five-spice powder is a blend of ground spices used extensively in Chinese cooking. It usually consists of cloves, cinnamon, fennel seed, star anise, and Szechwan peppercorns. It can be found in the spice section of the grocery store.

Southern Pulled Pork

servings 8 **prep time** 10 minutes
cooking time 7 to 8 hours (Low), 4 hours (High)

I created this down-home dish for an outdoor barbeque. Slow cooking blends Sloppy Joe mix, chili sauce, and beef broth into a simmered-in sauce that's uniquely tangy—leaving the meat so tender, it falls apart. Piled on buns, rolls, or on top of a salad, it's finger-lickin' fantastic!

- 2 tablespoons vegetable oil, *Wesson*®
- 1 pork shoulder roast (3½ pounds)
  Garlic salt
  Lemon pepper
- 1 bottle (12-ounce) chili sauce, *Del Monte*®
- 3 packets (1.31 ounces each) Sloppy Joe mix, *McCormick*®
- ½ cup low-sodium beef broth, *Swanson*®
  Hamburger buns

1. Heat oil in a large skillet over medium-high heat. Season pork roast with garlic salt and lemon pepper. Brown on all sides. Place in a 4- to 5-quart slow cooker.

2. In a small bowl, combine chili sauce, Sloppy Joe mix, and broth. Pour over roast.

3. Cover and cook on low-heat setting for 7 to 8 hours or high-heat setting for 4 hours. To serve, shred pork and place on hamburger buns.

Mushroom Risotto

servings 8 **prep time** 10 minutes
cooking time 2 hours, plus 30 minutes to 1 hour (High)

2	cups Arborio rice
1	cup white wine, *Vendage*®
4	cups vegetable broth, *Swanson*®
1	can (10¾-ounce) condensed cream of mushroom soup, *Campbell's*®
1	can (10¾-ounce) condensed golden mushroom soup, *Campbell's*®
1	teaspoon bottled minced garlic, *McCormick*®
6	ounces mushrooms, sliced
1	teaspoon salt
¼	teaspoon pepper
½	teaspoon dried thyme, *McCormick*®
½	cup grated Parmesan cheese, *Kraft*®
	Fresh thyme sprigs (optional)

1. Stir together Arborio rice, wine, vegetable broth, cream of mushroom soup, golden mushroom soup, garlic, mushrooms, salt, pepper, and dried thyme in a 4- to 5-quart slow cooker. Cook on high-heat setting for 2 hours, stirring every 30 minutes.

2. Check consistency. If necessary, continue to cook for an additional 30 minutes to 1 hour, stirring every 10 to 15 minutes. Be careful not to overcook risotto. (Rice should be *al dente*, not mushy.) Before serving, stir in Parmesan cheese and garnish with a sprig of fresh thyme (optional).

Turkey Meatballs in Marinara

servings 6 **prep time** 15 minutes
cooking time 8 to 9 hours (Low), 3 to 4 hours (High)

Whenever I'm hosting a party, I always serve meatballs—no matter how sophisticated the crowd, they're the first food to go. Serve meatballs on toothpicks for an easy-eat appetizer or layer over noodles for a homey meal. Diced and seasoned canned tomatoes add a spicy zing, while ground turkey makes them a healthful choice.

$1\frac{1}{2}$ **pounds ground turkey**
$1\frac{1}{4}$ **cups Italian bread crumbs,** *Progresso®*
$\frac{1}{4}$ **cup minced onion**
1 **teaspoon bottled minced garlic,** *McCormick®*
$\frac{1}{4}$ **cup chopped fresh parsley**
1 **egg, lightly beaten**
 Salt and pepper
1 **jar (26-ounce) marinara sauce,** *Prego®*
2 **cans (14.5 ounces each) diced tomatoes with basil, garlic, and oregano,** *Hunt's®*
2 **teaspoons dried basil,** *McCormick®*

1. In a medium bowl, combine ground turkey, bread crumbs, onion, garlic, parsley, egg, and salt and pepper. With your hands, blend ingredients together and form approximately thirty 1-inch meatballs. Set aside.

2. Clean the medium bowl and stir together marinara sauce, tomatoes, and dried basil. Pour half of sauce mixture into a 4- to 5-quart slow cooker. Add meatballs and top with remaining sauce. Cover and cook on low-heat setting for 8 to 9 hours or high-heat setting for 3 to 4 hours.

Hot Honeyed Spareribs

makes 12 appetizer portions **prep time** 15 minutes
cooking time 8 hours (Low), 3 to 4 hours (High)

Nonstick vegetable cooking spray, *PAM*®
4   pounds baby back ribs, cut into individual rib portions
     Garlic salt
     Black pepper
½   cup honey, *Sue Bee*®
¼   cup low-sodium soy sauce, *Kikkoman*®
¼   cup chili garlic sauce, *Sun Luck*®
1   cup Catalina dressing
1   teaspoon ground ginger, *McCormick*®

1. Preheat broiler. Line bottom portion of broiler pan with foil for easy cleanup. Spray top portion of broiler pan lightly with nonstick cooking spray.

2. Season cut ribs with garlic salt and pepper. Broil for 5 minutes. Turn and broil for an additional 5 minutes. Place browned ribs in a 4- to 5-quart slow cooker.

3. In a medium bowl, stir together honey, soy sauce, chili garlic sauce, Catalina dressing, and ginger. Pour sauce mixture over ribs. Move ribs around to make sure they are all coated. Cover and cook on low-heat setting for 8 hours or high-heat setting for 3 to 4 hours.

4. With tongs, remove ribs from slow cooker. Skim fat from sauce. Serve ribs with sauce on the side.

Five-Bean Chili

servings 8 **prep time** 15 minutes
cooking time 7 to 8 hours (Low), 4 hours (High)

1½ pounds lean ground beef
2 cups chopped onion
1 can (15-ounce) light red kidney beans
1 can (15-ounce) dark red kidney beans
1 can (15-ounce) cannellini beans
1 can (15-ounce) butter beans, drained
1 can (15-ounce) pinto beans, drained
2 cans (14.5 ounces each) diced tomatoes with chiles, *Hunt's®*
2 packets (1.25 ounces each) chili seasoning mix, *McCormick®*
½ cup tomato sauce, *Hunt's®*
  Salt and pepper
  Chili fixings: sliced green onion, shredded cheddar cheese, and/or sour cream (optional)

1. In a skillet over medium-high heat, brown ground beef with the onions. Drain fat and add meat to a 4- to 5-quart slow cooker.

2. Add light and dark kidney beans, cannellini beans, butter beans, pinto beans, tomatoes, chili seasoning mix, and tomato sauce to slow cooker and stir together. Cover and cook on low-heat setting for 7 to 8 hours or high-heat setting for 4 hours. Season to taste with salt and pepper.

3. Ladle into bowls; serve with chili fixings (optional) and corn bread.

Snacks

Snacking is a great American pastime. In fact, a recent *USA Today* Snapshot® poll asking "Where do you like to snack?" found that over 80 percent of us prefer to snack at home. This is why it's so important to be creative with our noshing foods. Most of us tend to feel a bit guilty about snacking between meals—however, it's been proven that eating certain foods between meals is actually good for us and can ultimately reduce the total amount of food we consume. Regular, healthful snacks are especially important for high-energy people, people with weight issues, and growing children.

Snacks are perfect energy boosters for kids at the end of the school day and before homework or chores. Snacks can add fun when bringing the family together to watch television or to play a board game. They can provide comfort on a cold winter's day and relief on a hot summer's day. Snacks are ideal to serve to friends and family who visit and great for boosting camaraderie among coworkers.

The Recipes

Caramel Popcorn

makes about 10 cups **prep time** 5 minutes
cooking time 1 hour **cooling time** 20 minutes

So sweet and crunchy, this popcorn will be gobbled up before the bowl hits the table. At our house, we serve individual bowls so everyone is assured of getting a fair share. As this is a great gift to give in bags or tins, remember to include a copy of the recipe. Everyone loves homemade goodies.

	Nonstick vegetable cooking spray, *PAM*®
3	bags (2.85 ounces each) microwave popcorn (no salt or butter), *Newman's Own*®
1	stick butter
1	cup (packed) golden brown sugar, *C&H*®
2/3	cup light corn syrup, *Karo*®
1	teaspoon baking soda, *Arm & Hammer*®

1. Preheat oven to 300 degrees F. Spray 2 large cookie sheets with nonstick spray.

2. Microwave popcorn according to package instructions. Place the popcorn into a very large bowl or roasting pan. Set aside.

3. In a 2-quart saucepan over medium heat, stir butter, sugar, and corn syrup until butter is melted and sugar dissolves. Bring to a boil and cook 4 minutes without stirring. Remove from heat and add baking soda to caramel sauce (mixture will foam).

4. Drizzle caramel sauce evenly over popcorn. Using 2 wooden spoons, toss popcorn to coat evenly with caramel sauce (popcorn will deflate somewhat).

5. Spread caramel corn in an even layer on each prepared cookie sheet. Bake until caramel corn is almost crisp, stirring every 15 minutes, for a total of 45 minutes. (Rotate pans halfway through baking.)

6. Using a metal spatula, loosen caramel corn from cookie sheets. Cool caramel corn completely.

Storage and Leftovers: Store in an airtight container at room temperature for up to 7 days.

Tortelloni and Ravioli Bites

servings 10 **prep time** 5 minutes
cooking time 5 minutes

1   package (9-ounce) assorted tortelloni (refrigerated section), *Buitoni®*
1   package (9-ounce) assorted ravioli (refrigerated section), *Buitoni®*
1   container (7-ounce) pesto sauce, *Buitoni®*
1   container (10-ounce) Alfredo sauce, *Buitoni®*
    Skewers or toothpicks

1. Prepare tortelloni and ravioli according to package instructions. Arrange both pastas on the same platter in a decorative fashion (by color or shape).

2. Heat pesto and Alfredo sauces separately and serve on the side. Serve pasta with toothpicks or small skewers for dipping into sauces.

Healthful Onion Rings

servings 4 **prep time** 8 minutes
cooking time 30 minutes

    Nonstick vegetable cooking spray, *PAM®*
1   large onion
1¼ cups Italian-style bread crumbs, *Progresso®*
½   teaspoon bottled minced garlic, *McCormick®*
1   cup low-fat milk
1   cup all-purpose flour, *Pillsbury®*
3   large egg whites, lightly beaten

1. Preheat oven to 400 degrees F. Spray 2 large cookie sheets with nonstick spray.

2. Cut onion into ½-inch slices. Separate slices into rings.

3. In a small bowl, combine bread crumbs and garlic. Set aside.

4. Place milk, flour, and egg whites into 3 separate small bowls. Dip each onion ring into milk, flour, egg white, and bread crumbs (in that order).

5. Place on prepared cookie sheets and bake for 20 minutes. Turn onion rings over and bake until golden brown, about 10 minutes longer.

Mini Biscuit Pizzas

servings 6 **prep time** 10 minutes
cooking time 20 minutes

Mini pizzas are always popular—they make fantastic finger foods for family and friends. Fun to make and quick to clean up, they're great for after-school snacks, rainy-day treats, or as just a little something to tide you over.

3   containers (16.3 ounces each) refrigerated prepared buttermilk biscuit dough, *Pillsbury® Grands!®*
    Nonstick vegetable cooking spray, *PAM®*
1   cup chopped onion
1   package (3-ounce) thinly sliced prosciutto (deli section), chopped, *Citterio®*
1   cup traditional tomato sauce, *Ragū®*
6   large button mushrooms, sliced
1   cup shredded pizza-blend cheese, *Sargento®*

1. Bake biscuits according to package instructions. Cool biscuits.

2. Spray cookie sheet with nonstick spray. Split biscuits in half and arrange, split sides up, on cookie sheet. Set aside. Bring oven heat to 400 degrees F.

3. In a small bowl, combine onion and prosciutto. In a second small bowl, combine tomato sauce and mushrooms. Spread tomato mixture evenly over biscuit halves. Sprinkle with cheese. Top with prosciutto and onion mixture.

4. Bake for 12 minutes or until topping is golden brown. Serve warm.

Bagel Chip Dip

servings 6
prep time 5 minutes

1   container (16-ounce) sour cream
1   cup finely chopped green onions
3/4 cup mayonnaise, *Best Foods®* or *Hellmann's®*
1/4 cup chopped fresh parsley
3   tablespoons chopped fresh dill
2   teaspoons seasoned salt, *Lawry's®*
2   bags bagel chips, *Bagel Crisps®*

1. In a medium bowl, combine sour cream, green onions, mayonnaise, parsley, dill, and seasoned salt. Serve dip with bagel chips.

Storage and Leftovers: Cover tightly and store Chip Dip in refrigerator for up to 2 days.

Banana Grape-Nuts® Chews

makes 24 cookies **prep time** 10 minutes
cooking time 12 minutes per batch

Nonstick vegetable cooking spray, *PAM®*
6   tablespoons (3/4 stick) butter
1/3 cup packed golden brown sugar, *C&H®*
2   teaspoons ground cinnamon, *McCormick®*
2   egg yolks
1 1/2 cups banana quick bread mix, *Betty Crocker®*
1   cup *Grape-Nuts®* cereal, *Post®*
2   bananas, peeled and coarsely mashed (about 1 cup)

1. Position rack in center of oven and preheat to 375 degrees F. Spray large cookie sheet with nonstick spray.

2. Using an electric mixer, beat butter, brown sugar, and cinnamon in large bowl until fluffy. Beat in yolks one at a time. Add quick bread mix and cereal and beat until just blended. Add mashed bananas and beat just to incorporate.

3. Working in batches, spoon 2 tablespoons batter for each cookie onto prepared cookie sheet, spacing evenly and forming 6 mounds.

4. Bake until cookies are golden brown on bottom and set in the middle, about 12 minutes. Using a spatula, transfer cookies to cooling rack. Repeat with remaining cookie dough.

Storage and Leftovers: Cover tightly and store at room temperature for up to 3 days.

Hummus Pitas

servings 4 **prep time** 8 minutes
cooking time 10 minutes

Until now, I'd never tasted a hummus I liked. In fact, before this recipe, I would have sworn to you I hated hummus—but no more. This particular combination is delicious: If you're already a hummus fan, you'll be thrilled; if you're hesitant, this will surely win your heart.

4   pita pockets, each cut into 4 wedges, *Mr.Pita®*
    Olive oil cooking spray, *PAM®*
    Salt and pepper
1   large garlic clove
1   can (15.5-ounce) garbanzo beans, drained, *S&W®*
3   tablespoons sour cream
3   tablespoons fresh lemon juice, or *ReaLemon®*
1/2 teaspoon salt
1/4 teaspoon ground cumin, *McCormick®*
1/4 cup extra-virgin olive oil, *Bertolli®*

1. Preheat oven to 400 degrees F. Arrange pita wedges in a single layer on a large cookie sheet. Spray wedges generously with olive oil cooking spray. Sprinkle with salt and pepper. Bake 5 minutes. Turn wedges over. Spray wedges again with olive oil cooking spray. Bake until wedges are golden brown and crisp, about 5 minutes longer. Cool completely.

2. Meanwhile, finely mince garlic in work bowl of a food processor. Add beans, sour cream, lemon juice, salt, and cumin. Process until almost smooth. With machine running, gradually add oil through feed tube. Process until mixture is smooth, scraping down sides of work bowl occasionally. Transfer hummus to bowl. Serve with pita chips.

Storage and Leftovers: Cover hummus tightly and store in refrigerator for up to 2 days. Bake fresh pita wedges when re-serving.

Stuffed Crescents

servings 8 **prep time** 10 minutes
cooking time 20 minutes

1   container (8-ounce) refrigerated crescent roll dough, *Pillsbury*®
6   tablespoons shredded sharp cheddar cheese, *Kraft*®
6   tablespoons shredded Parmesan cheese, *Kraft*®
6   tablespoons onion-flavored cheese spread, *Boursin*®

1. Preheat oven to 350 degrees F. Lay dough for each crescent roll flat on a clean surface. Fill each of 3 rolls with 2 tablespoons cheddar cheese, each of 2 rolls with 3 tablespoons Parmesan cheese, each of 3 rolls with 2 tablespoons cheese spread. Roll up each crescent to enclose filling.

2. Place, seam sides down, onto a cookie sheet. Bake for 20 minutes or until cooked thoroughly and golden on top. Cut each roll in half and serve hot.

Bursting Blueberry Snacks

servings 8 **prep time** 10 minutes
freezing time 1 hour

1   bag (16-ounce) frozen unsweetened blueberries, thawed
1/2   cup pitted dates, *Sun-Maid*®
1   cup *Grape-Nuts*® cereal, *Post*®
2   large ripe bananas, peeled and sliced
1/2   cup raisins, *Sun-Maid*®

1. Place blueberries into a blender and pulse for 1 minute. Gradually add dates and blend until almost smooth.

2. In each of eight 6-ounce custard cups or glass bowls, add 2 tablespoons cereal to line bottom. Spoon 3 tablespoons blueberry mixture into each cup. Arrange sliced bananas on top of mixture. Sprinkle with raisins. Cover with remaining blueberry mixture. Freeze 1 hour.

3. Run small sharp knife around cups to loosen fruit mixture. Invert cups onto plates and serve.

Desserts

Like most people, I love desserts—they're my weakness. Growing up, I would sit in the kitchen for hours and watch my grandmother bake and decorate the most fabulous cakes. Unfortunately, none of us has time for this luxurious expression of love anymore. To this day, I have not forgotten my grandmother's greatest creations—her famous dessert casseroles. None of us ever knew exactly what was in them, but our mouths watered in anticipation of every bite. Now I, too, have continued her not-so-common tradition. Even my grandmother would take her hat off to the wonderful desserts included here. My decadent treats are not as time-consuming as the old-fashioned delicacies, but I promise you they are just as amazing, and only you will know how truly easy they are to make.

The Recipes

Banana Purse

makes 12 purses **prep time** 10 minutes
cooking time 15 minutes

Nonstick vegetable cooking spray, *PAM*®
3   bananas, peeled and thinly sliced
1/4   cup maple-flavored pancake syrup, *Log Cabin Original Syrup*®
1   package (2 sheets) frozen puff pastry, thawed, *Pepperidge Farm*®
1   tablespoon granulated sugar, *C&H*®
1   teaspoon ground cinnamon, *McCormick*®
2   tablespoons whole milk

1. Position rack in center of oven and preheat to 400 degrees F. Line a large heavy cookie sheet with foil. Spray foil with nonstick spray.

2. In a medium bowl, combine bananas and syrup. Mash bananas slightly with a fork. Divide banana mixture in half.

3. On a clean surface, lay flat 1 sheet of puff pastry. Cut pastry in half lengthwise. Using a rolling pin, roll out each pastry sheet into a 15×5-inch rectangle. Cut each rectangle crosswise into thirds, forming 6 squares total.

4. Using half of the banana mixture, evenly divide banana mixture onto center of each square. Fold corners of pastry into center and pinch ends together, twisting to seal. Repeat with remaining sheet of puff pastry and banana mixture. Arrange pastries on prepared cookie sheet.

5. In a small bowl, combine sugar and cinnamon. Brush pastries with milk. Sprinkle cinnamon-sugar over pastries. Bake for 15 minutes or until golden. Serve warm.

Raspberry Trifle with Rum Sauce

servings 6 **prep time** 10 minutes
cooking time 1 minute
cooling time 45 minutes

Visually glorious and equally matched in flavor, this trifle is outrageously delicious and undoubtedly one of the most beautiful photographs we shot for this book. The entire crew admitted their mouths were watering, and so will yours once you taste it. Sinful!

3	tablespoons butter
¾	cup powdered sugar, *C&H®*
¾	teaspoon imitation rum extract, *McCormick®*
3	tablespoons water
½	cup raspberry jam, *Knott's Berry Farm®*
1	frozen pound cake (12-ounce), thawed and cut into quarter-size cubes, *Sara Lee®*
3	containers (4 ounces each) refrigerated prepared vanilla pudding, *Jell-O®*
	Fresh raspberries

1. Heat butter in a large glass bowl in microwave on high until melted, about 30 seconds. Whisk in powdered sugar, rum extract, water, and jam, stirring to form a smooth sauce.

2. In 6 small bowls or wineglasses, evenly distribute pound cake cubes. Pack cubes down slightly. Drizzle jam-rum sauce evenly over each. Spoon 3 tablespoons of pudding evenly over each.

3. Serve warm or refrigerate for 45 minutes. Garnish with raspberries and serve.

Malibu® Rum Cake

servings 12 **prep time** 8 minutes
cooking time 45 minutes **cooling time** 45 minutes

I created this cake in college, and it was always a big hit. I wonder if having the word "rum" in its title added to its success?

Cake

	Nonstick vegetable cooking spray, *PAM*®
1	package (18.25-ounce) classic yellow cake mix, *Duncan Hines Moist Deluxe*®
1	cup *Malibu*® Rum
¹/₂	cup vegetable oil, *Wesson*®
1	package (3.4-ounce) vanilla instant pudding and pie filling mix, *Jell-O*®
4	eggs

Rum Glaze:

1	cup packed golden brown sugar, *C&H*®
¹/₄	cup water
1	stick butter
¹/₄	cup *Malibu*® Rum

Cake Preparation

1. Position rack in center of oven and preheat to 325 degrees F. Spray a 10-inch (12-cup) Bundt pan with nonstick cooking spray.

2. Using an electric mixer, beat all the cake ingredients in a large bowl for 2 minutes. Transfer batter to prepared pan. Bake until a toothpick inserted into center of cake comes out clean, about 45 minutes.

3. Cool cake in pan for 20 minutes. Invert cake onto platter, then carefully remove pan. Allow cake to cool completely.

Rum Glaze Preparation

4. Meanwhile, stir sugar and water in a medium heavy saucepan over medium-high heat until sugar dissolves. Add butter. Simmer until mixture thickens and is syrupy, stirring often, about 5 minutes.

5. Remove saucepan from heat and whisk in rum. Cool glaze completely. Drizzle glaze evenly over cooled cake and serve.

Storage and Leftovers: Cover tightly and store rum cake at room temperature for up to 3 days. Cover tightly and store rum glaze in refrigerator for up to 3 days. Best served at room temperature.

Vanilla Cream Pie

servings 6 to 8 **prep time** 15 minutes
cooking time 20 minutes **cooling time** 1 hour

Did you know that bananas are among the most frequently purchased items in grocery stores? Who would have guessed? I've been enjoying this wonderful dessert since I was ten, and I still love it as much as I did then.

1   burrito-size (10-inch) flour tortilla, *Mission®*
2   tablespoons butter, melted
2   tablespoons granulated sugar, *C&H®*
2   ripe bananas, peeled
2   containers (4 ounces each) refrigerated prepared
      vanilla pudding, *Jell-O®*
1   teaspoon vanilla extract, *McCormick®*
1   container (8-ounce) frozen whipped topping, thawed, *Cool Whip®*

1. Preheat oven to 325 degrees F. Generously brush both sides of the tortilla with melted butter. Sprinkle 1 side of tortilla with sugar. Line a 9-inch pie pan with tortilla, sugared side up.

2. Bake until tortilla is crisp and golden, about 20 minutes. Cool crust completely.

3. Cut bananas crosswise into $\frac{1}{4}$-inch-thick slices. Mix pudding and vanilla extract in medium bowl to blend. Fold in 1 cup whipped topping. Fold in banana slices. Transfer mixture to prepared tortilla crust. Cover pie tightly and refrigerate at least 1 hour or up to 8 hours.

4. Cut pie into wedges. Top wedges with remaining whipped topping.

Berry Cookie Cobbler

servings 8 **prep time** 5 minutes
cooking time 45 minutes

This is easy, easy, easy—delicious, delicious, delicious. *Today show's* Ann Curry high-fived me live on-air when she tasted it—it's truly that good. You'll look and feel like a professional baker when this beautiful dessert comes out of the oven. If the filling bubbles over a bit in baking, leave it (it adds a mouthwatering appeal). I let it cool just a little and serve it with a scoop of vanilla ice cream. Yum.

2   bags (12 ounces each) frozen mixed berries, thawed
1   container (21-ounce) apple pie filling, *Comstock*®
1/3   cup granulated sugar, *C&H*®
1½   teaspoons ground cinnamon, *McCormick*®
1   package (18-ounce) refrigerated sugar cookie dough, *Pillsbury*®
       Vanilla ice cream, *Dreyer's*® or *Edy's*®

1. Preheat oven to 350 degrees F. In a large bowl, mix berries, apple pie filling, sugar, and cinnamon. Transfer fruit mixture to an 8×8×2-inch baking dish. Crumble the cookie dough over fruit, covering thickly and completely.

2. Bake, uncovered, until cookie crust is golden and crisp and juices bubble thickly, about 45 minutes. Serve warm with ice cream.

Ricotta Berry Bursts

makes 6 tartlets **prep time** 10 minutes
cooking time 5 minutes

Make this as soon as possible! So smooth and creamy, it's packed with the most wonderful burst of berry flavor.

1	package (4-ounce) 6 mini graham cracker crusts, *Keebler®*
1	egg white
³/₄	cup boysenberry jam, *Knott's Berry Farm®*
1	container (14-ounce) whole-milk ricotta
1	tablespoon orange juice, *Minute Maid®*
	Fresh boysenberries or blackberries (optional)

1. Preheat oven to 375 degrees F. Brush crusts with egg white. Bake until golden, about 5 minutes. Cool crusts completely.

2. Melt ¹/₄ cup of the jam in a small glass bowl in microwave on high, about 30 seconds. Spoon 2 teaspoons melted jam over bottom of each crust.

3. Blend remaining ¹/₂ cup jam, ricotta, and orange juice in blender until smooth. Divide mixture among crusts.

4. Serve immediately or cover tightly and refrigerate up to 8 hours. Garnish with fresh berries (optional).

Cream Cheese Flan

servings 8 **prep time** 5 minutes
cooking time 1 hour **cooling time** 4 hours

1   **cup granulated sugar, *C&H*®**
¼   **cup water**
1   **can (14-ounce) sweetened condensed milk, *Carnation*®**
1   **package (8-ounce) cream cheese, softened, *Philadelphia*®**
5   **eggs**
1   **teaspoon vanilla extract, *McCormick*®**
1   **can (12-ounce) evaporated milk, *Carnation*®**

1. Position rack in center of oven and preheat to 350 degrees F. Arrange eight 6-ounce oven-safe custard or dessert cups in a large heavy roasting pan.

2. Stir sugar and water in a small heavy saucepan over low heat until sugar dissolves. Increase heat to high and boil without stirring until the liquid is a deep golden brown, brushing down sides of saucepan with a wet pastry brush to prevent sugar from crystallizing, about 12 minutes. Quickly pour syrup into prepared cups.

3. In a blender, combine condensed milk, cream cheese, eggs, and vanilla. Blend until just smooth, about 30 seconds. Transfer to an 8-cup measuring cup or large bowl. Whisk in evaporated milk. Divide custard equally among prepared cups.

4. Transfer roasting pan to oven. Pour enough water into roasting pan to come halfway up the sides of the custard cups. Bake until sides are firmly set and centers of custards jiggle slightly when cups are gently shaken, about 45 minutes (custards will firm up as they cool).

5. Remove cups from pan, cover tightly with aluminum foil, and refrigerate until cold, at least 4 hours and up to 24 hours.

6. Run small sharp knife around sides of custards. Invert each cup onto a dessert plate, shaking gently to release custard from cups. Drizzle syrup remaining in pan over custard. Serve cold.

Note: If necessary, rewarm cups in microwave to melt sugar syrup. If desired, garnish flans with fresh berries.

Gooey Mud Pie

servings 8 **prep time** 20 minutes
freezing time 1 hour 45 minutes

1   jar (11.75-ounce) hot fudge topping, slightly warm, *Smucker's*®
1   9-inch premade chocolate piecrust, *Keebler*®
1   quart coffee ice cream, *Dreyer's*® or *Edy's*®
1   cup frozen light whipped topping, thawed, *Cool Whip*®
1   bottle (7.25-ounce) chocolate shell topping, *Smucker's*® *Magic Shell*®

1. Drizzle half of the warm fudge topping over bottom of piecrust. Spoon half of the ice cream in an even layer over fudge topping. Drizzle remaining fudge topping over ice cream. Freeze pie for 15 minutes.

2. Using a wooden spoon, stir remaining half of ice cream in a large bowl to loosen. Stir in $1/4$ cup whipped topping. Fold in remaining whipped topping to create a mousselike texture.

3. Spoon mixture onto fudge-topped ice cream layer. Freeze until firm, at least 1 hour. Drizzle $1/4$ of the chocolate topping over top of pie. Freeze pie 5 minutes. Repeat drizzling and freezing 3 more times. Cut pie into wedges and serve immediately.

Storage and Leftovers: Cover tightly and freeze for up to 3 days.

Marbled Sour Cream Cake

servings 8 to 10 **prep time** 10 minutes
cooking time 55 minutes
cooling time 30 minutes

Nonstick vegetable cooking spray, *PAM*®
1 cup semisweet chocolate morsels, *Hershey's*®
1 package (18.25-ounce) yellow cake mix, *Betty Crocker Super Moist*®
1 cup sour cream
1 cup water
¾ cup vegetable oil, *Wesson*®
¾ cup granulated sugar, *C&H*®
4 eggs

1. Position rack in center of oven and preheat to 375 degrees F. Spray a 10-inch (12-cup) Bundt pan with nonstick cooking spray.

2. In a medium glass bowl, microwave chocolate morsels on high for 30 seconds. Stir to blend. Continue to microwave until morsels are melted and smooth, about 30 seconds longer. Set aside.

3. In a large bowl, combine cake mix, sour cream, water, oil, sugar, and eggs. Using an electric mixer, beat until very well blended, about 2 minutes.

4. Spoon 2 cups of cake batter into melted chocolate, then mix thoroughly to form chocolate batter. Spoon chocolate batter and yellow batter alternately into prepared pan.

5. Bake until a toothpick inserted into center of cake comes out clean, about 55 minutes. Transfer pan to a cooling rack and cool completely, or refrigerate for 30 minutes. Invert cake onto a platter, then carefully remove pan.

Storage and Leftovers: Cover tightly and store at room temperature for up to 3 days.

Kahlúa® Tiramisu

servings 6 **prep time** 10 minutes
cooling time 30 minutes

After reading all of these wonderful dessert recipes, you may think I'm a spokesperson for Cool Whip®—however, I just happen to be a huge fan. The reason I like to use Cool Whip® is simple: I think it's one of the best-tasting premade products on the market, and its consistency is incredible for cooking! Pure perfection for topping off my Kahlúa® Tiramisu and the only thing I use in creating a *Semi-Homemade* mousse. Serve this dessert after dinner with coffee, at an afternoon tea, or anytime, really. You're in for a wonderful treat.

- 12 teaspoons plus 2 tablespoons *Kahlúa*®
- 18 soft ladyfingers (available in the packaged baked goods section)
- 1 container (8-ounce) mascarpone cheese, softened
- 1 tablespoon granulated sugar, *C&H*®
- 3 containers (4 ounces each) refrigerated prepared
      vanilla pudding, *Jell-O*®
- 6 teaspoons frozen whipped topping, thawed, *Cool Whip*®
   Cocoa powder, *Hershey's*®

1. Line six 1-cup glass custard cups with plastic wrap. Spoon 2 teaspoons Kahlúa® into each cup. Soak 3 ladyfingers in each cup, turning to coat both sides. Arrange lady fingers around sides of cups. Set aside.

2. In a large bowl, whisk mascarpone, sugar, and remaining 2 tablespoons Kahlúa® until just smooth. Whisk in pudding.

3. Divide pudding mixture equally among prepared cups. Cover tightly and refrigerate until set, about 30 minutes or up to 1 day.

4. Uncover cups. Invert cups onto plates and remove plastic wrap. Top each with 1 teaspoon whipped topping and sprinkle with cocoa powder just before serving.

Bananas Foster Pies

makes 12 mini pies **prep time** 13 minutes
cooking time 10 minutes

These mini pies will melt in your mouth. They're sensational! Make a couple extra and save them for yourself. A few indulgences never hurt anyone.

2   packages (4 ounces each) 6 mini graham cracker crusts, *Keebler*®
1   egg white, lightly beaten
1   cup packed golden brown sugar, *C&H*®
1   stick butter, cut into pieces
¼   cup brandy, *Christian Brothers*®
6   bananas, peeled and thinly sliced
    Vanilla ice cream, *Dreyer's*® or *Edy's*®
    Frozen whipped topping, thawed, *Cool Whip*®

1. Preheat oven to 375 degrees F. Arrange piecrusts (in pie tins) on a large cookie sheet. Brush crusts with egg white. Bake until crusts are golden, about 5 minutes.

2. In a medium heavy saucepan, heat brown sugar and butter over medium heat until butter melts; whisk until mixture is creamy, about 3 minutes. Whisk in brandy. Remove from heat. Stir in bananas. Let stand 5 minutes.

3. Divide banana mixture equally among piecrusts. Serve with ice cream and whipped topping.

Gravies and Sauces

Have you ever wondered how to change the flavor of an ordinary meal? How about fixing the taste of something you've overcooked? Are you bored with meatloaf and pasta? Does one more night of "rubber chicken" make you want to go squawking out of the kitchen? Before you fly the coop, you should know that I am an expert at livening up the old standbys. What is the answer? Gravies and sauces. Many people find making a gravy or sauce to be a challenge, but I have learned it's the easiest thing to do with a little know-how. My family lovingly dubbed me the "Gravy Queen." I can show you how to camouflage any imperfection, whether it's in presentation or taste.

Here are some secrets to giving the old food you fancy a new flavor. Whether you are serving red meat, fish, poultry, or pasta, you'll find a recipe that will make any dish delicious.

The Recipes

Creamy Mustard Sauce

makes 1½ cups **prep time** 3 minutes
cooking time 1 minute

Near my house is a small French café called La Conversation. In the evening, they serve pork roast smothered in a mustard-based sauce. I eat every bite—it's so good. Since they won't share their secret recipe, I've created a similar sauce. Put it on any meat, fish, or fowl.

1	cup heavy cream
½	cup Dijon mustard, *French's*®
	Pinch of ground white pepper, *McCormick*®
	Salt

1. In a small saucepan, mix cream, mustard, and pepper. Simmer until sauce thickens slightly, stirring constantly, about 1 minute. Season to taste with salt. Serve over pork, ham, chicken, steamed vegetables, potatoes, or rice.

Storage and Leftovers: Cover tightly and store in refrigerator for up to 2 days. Reheat in a saucepan over low heat, stirring frequently until warm.

More-Than-Meatloaf Gravy

makes 2 cups **prep time** 2 minutes **cooking time** 8 minutes

1	tablespoon canola oil, *Wesson*®
1	tablespoon all-purpose flour, *Pillsbury*®
1	can (14-ounce) beef broth, *Swanson*®
1/4	cup tomato sauce, *Hunt's*®
1	package (1.2-ounce) brown gravy mix, *Knorr*®
	Salt and pepper

1. In a medium frying pan over medium heat, warm oil. Add flour and stir to form a paste. Let paste cook until it is a deep golden brown, about 2 minutes. Whisk in broth, tomato sauce, and gravy mix. Simmer until sauce thickens slightly, about 5 minutes.

2. Season to taste with salt and pepper. Serve over meatloaf, meatballs, beef, veal, potatoes, or rice.

Easy Warm Pesto

makes 1 3/4 cups **prep time** 5 minutes
cooking time 2 minutes (microwave)

2	cups (packed) fresh basil leaves
1	cup pine nuts, *Diamond*®
3	tablespoons bottled minced garlic, *McCormick*®
3/4	cup shredded Parmesan cheese, *Kraft*®
3/4	cup olive oil, *Bertolli*®

1. Place basil leaves, pine nuts, and garlic into work bowl of a food processor. Pulse until paste forms, about 1 minute. Add cheese and olive oil and pulse until mixture is smooth.

2. Place in microwave-safe bowl. Cook on medium heat for 2 minutes or just until hot, stirring after 1 minute. Serve over chicken, veal, seafood, or pasta.

Sherry Mushroom Gravy

makes 2 cups **prep time** 5 minutes **cooling time** 5 minutes

1	can (10 3/4-ounce) cream of mushroom soup, *Campbell's*®
3/4	cup canned reduced-sodium beef broth, *Swanson*®
1/4	cup dry sherry, *Christian Brothers*®
	Salt and pepper

1. Blend soup, broth, and sherry in a blender until smooth. Transfer mixture to a medium heavy saucepan. Bring sauce to simmer over medium-high heat. Stir until sauce thickens slightly, about 2 minutes.

2. Season to taste with salt and pepper. Serve over steaks, chops, beef, turkey, or veggie burgers, omelets, potatoes, or rice.

Storage and Leftovers: All of the gravies and sauces should be covered tightly and stored in refrigerator for up to 2 days. Reheat in a saucepan over low heat, stirring frequently until warm.

Clockwise from lower right: Sherry Mushroom Gravy, Easy Warm Pesto, More-Than-Meatloaf Gravy

Vegetable Cream Sauce

makes 2 cups **prep time** 2 minutes **cooking time** 5 minutes

1   can (10 $^3/_4$-ounce) cream of broccoli soup, *Campbell's*®
$^3/_4$ cup whole milk
1$^1/_2$ cups shredded sharp cheddar cheese, *Kraft*®
2   tablespoons chopped fresh chives
$^1/_2$ teaspoon bottled minced garlic, *McCormick*®
    Salt and pepper

1. Stir soup and milk in medium heavy saucepan over medium heat to blend. Bring to simmer. Gradually whisk in cheese and stir until melted. Stir in chives and garlic.

2. Season to taste with salt and pepper. Serve over broccoli, asparagus, cauliflower, or potatoes.

Ricotta Chive Sauce

makes 2 cups **prep time** 5 minutes **cooking time** 5 minutes

1   can (10-ounce) cream of chicken soup, *Campbell's*®
1   cup canned chicken broth, *Swanson*®
$^1/_2$ cup ricotta cheese (or small curd cottage cheese)
$^1/_4$ cup chopped fresh chives
    Pinch of ground nutmeg, *McCormick*®
    Salt and pepper

1. In a blender, place soup, broth, ricotta cheese, chives, and nutmeg. Pulse until smooth. Transfer mixture to a medium saucepan. Stir over medium heat until sauce simmers.

2. Season to taste with salt and pepper. Serve over noodles, rice, potatoes, or vegetables.

Blended Hollandaise Sauce

makes 1$^2/_3$ cups **prep time** 5 minutes

5   egg yolks
3   tablespoons fresh lemon juice, or *ReaLemon*®
$^1/_4$ teaspoon cayenne pepper, *McCormick*®
2   sticks butter, melted, hot

1. Into a blender, place yolks, lemon juice, and cayenne pepper. Pulse for 10 seconds. Add butter and pulse for 10 seconds.

2. Serve immediately over beef, chicken, eggs, omelets, potatoes, rice, turkey, or vegetables.

Storage and Leftovers: All of the gravies and sauces should be covered tightly and stored in refrigerator for up to 2 days. Reheat in a saucepan over low heat, stirring frequently until warm.

Clockwise from lower right: Vegetable Cream Sauce, Ricotta Chive Sauce, Blended Hollandaise Sauce

Horseradish Sour Cream Sauce

makes 1¾ cups **prep time** 2 minutes **cooking time** 5 minutes

- ½ cup whole milk
- 2 tablespoons prepared cream-style horseradish, *Silver Spring*®
- 1 teaspoon Dijon mustard, *French's*®
- ½ teaspoon ground white pepper, *McCormick*®
- ½ teaspoon salt
- 1 container (8-ounce) sour cream

1. In a medium saucepan over medium heat, stir milk, horseradish, mustard, white pepper, and salt. Simmer gently about 5 minutes.

2. Remove saucepan from heat. Whisk in sour cream. Serve over potatoes, vegetables, seafood, pork, or beef.

Garlic Chicken Gravy

makes 1½ cups **prep time** 3 minutes **cooking time** 10 minutes

- 2 tablespoons butter
- 1 teaspoon bottled minced garlic, *McCormick*®
- 2 tablespoons all-purpose flour, *Pillsbury*®
- 1 cup whole milk
- 1 cup canned chicken broth, *Swanson*®
- Salt and pepper

1. In a medium frying pan over medium heat, melt butter. Add garlic and saute 1 minute. Stir in flour to form a paste. Cook until golden brown, about 1 minute. Whisk in milk and broth. Simmer for 8 minutes until sauce thickens, whisking often.

2. Season to taste with salt and pepper. Serve over chicken, turkey, seafood, mashed potatoes, or rice.

Herbed Tomato Sauce

makes 2 cups **prep time** 3 minutes **cooking time** 5 minutes

- 1 jar (14-ounce) tomato and basil pasta sauce, *Classico*®
- 2 teaspoons Italian seasoning, *McCormick Classic Herbs*®
- ½ cup sour cream

1. In a medium saucepan, combine pasta sauce and seasoning. Cover and cook over medium heat, stirring occasionally, about 5 minutes.

2. Remove from heat. Whisk in sour cream. Serve over pasta, rice, vegetables, or potatoes.

Green Pepper Steak Gravy

makes 2 cups **prep time** 3 minutes **cooking time** 10 minutes

- 1 tablespoon canola oil, *Wesson*®
- 1 cup frozen pepper strips, thawed, *C&W*®
- 2 cups canned beef broth, *Swanson*®
- 2 tablespoons all-purpose flour, *Pillsbury*®
- 2 teaspoons Dijon mustard, *French's*®
- Salt and pepper

1. In a medium frying pan on medium-high heat, warm oil. Saute peppers until beginning to brown, about 3 minutes. Add 1 cup of the broth and bring to a simmer.

2. Place flour in a small bowl; gradually whisk in the remaining 1 cup of broth until flour is dissolved. Slowly pour flour mixture into pepper mixture, whisking vigorously. Simmer until mixture thickens, stirring occasionally, about 4 minutes. Stir in mustard. Reduce heat to low and simmer for 2 minutes longer.

3. Season sauce to taste with salt and pepper. Serve hot over beef, veal, pork, turkey, potatoes, or rice.

Storage and Leftovers: All of the gravies and sauces should be covered tightly and stored in refrigerator for up to 2 days. Reheat in a saucepan over low heat, stirring frequently until warm.

Clockwise from lower right: Horseradish Sour Cream Sauce, Garlic Chicken Gravy, Herbed Tomato Sauce, Green Pepper Steak Gravy

Kids' Cooking

Kids are notoriously picky eaters. Whipping up the perfect soufflé is nothing, compared to getting little ones to take a bite. If my nieces and nephews have taught me anything, it's that if they cook it, they'll eat it. Involving kids in the kitchen is not only fun for them; it's fun for adults, too—a cozy way to bring the family together while nurturing children's creativity and self-reliance.

Easy to make and easy to eat, these recipes can't miss with kids, serving up good-for-you food that keeps budding hungry chefs happy at breakfast, lunch, dinner, and snacks in between. The trick is to think differently, giving childhood favorites a grown-up twist—fish and chips in a cereal crust, funnel cake flavored with coffee creamer, or fruit punch with health-conscious cranberry. Mom-tested and kid-approved, they feed everybody's "inner chef," letting cooks of all sizes wield a spatula with ease.

The Recipes

Chefs-in-the-making Brycer, Austen, & Stephanie top off dinner with quick condiments in Aunt Sandy's kitchen.

Bunny Hotcakes with Apple Butter Cream

servings 4 **prep time** 20 minutes
cooking time 10 minutes

A few creative additions turn plain pancakes into a cute-as-a-bunny breakfast. Use one pancake for the face and a second to cut out ears and a bow tie. The icing on the cake—apple butter cream, garnished with licorice whiskers and chocolate chip eyes and nose. All kids say is "yum" and "yeah"!

2   cups just-add-water pancake mix, *Aunt Jemima Complete*®
1½ cups apple juice
1¼ teaspoons ground cinnamon, *McCormick*®
1   container (8-ounce) whipped cream cheese, *Philadelphia*®
⅔   cup apple butter
     Whipped cream cheese (optional)
     Nonstick cooking spray, *PAM*®
     Black licorice (optional)
     Large chocolate morsels, *Hershey's*® (optional)

1. In a medium mixing bowl, whisk together pancake mix, apple juice, and cinnamon. Set aside.

2. In a small mixing bowl, combine whipped cream cheese and apple butter until smooth. If desired, place additional whipped cream cheese in a self-sealing plastic bag. Snip a small corner from plastic bag and set aside.

3. Lightly spray a large skillet with nonstick cooking spray and heat over medium heat. Scoop pancake batter with ⅓ cup measure to make pancakes. Flip pancakes when they start to bubble. Cook an additional 1 to 2 minutes or until golden brown. Remove to cooling rack.

4. To make bunny, place 1 pancake in the center of the plate. On a cutting board, cut ears and bow tie from another pancake. Arrange to make bunny. Repeat with remaining pancakes.

5. Reheat hotcakes in microwave for 30 seconds to 1 minute. Spread with the apple butter mixture. Use the cream cheese in the plastic bag to pipe eyes, mouth, and a bow on the bunny. Decorate with licorice for whiskers and chocolate morsels for eyes and nose.

Pillow Dogs

1   package (1-pound) miniature beef cocktail wieners (48-count)
1   container (16.3-ounce) prepared buttermilk biscuit dough,
      Pillsbury® Grands!®
1   cup shredded sharp cheddar cheese, *Kraft®*
    Mustard (optional)

1. Preheat oven to 375 degrees F. Line a sheet pan with parchment paper or foil. In a grill pan on medium heat, cook cocktail wieners in 2 batches until plump, about 5 minutes. Set aside.

2. On a clean surface, cut the 8 large biscuits into sixths. Place cheese in a small bowl and roll each slice of dough in the cheese to make little cheese balls. Gently stretch each ball to fit a mini cocktail wiener. Partially wrap the dough around the mini cocktail wiener.

3. Arrange pillow dogs on prepared sheet pan. Leave about 1-inch space between each roll. Bake for 10 minutes. Top with mustard or other desired condiments. Serve warm.

Hamburger Dogs

1¼ pounds ground beef
1   packet (1.5-ounce) meatloaf seasoning, *McCormick®*
2   tablespoons ketchup
¼   cup bread crumbs, *Progresso®*
1   egg
    Hot dog buns
    Ketchup, relish, and chopped onions (optional)

1. Preheat grill to medium-high heat.

2. In a large bowl, combine ground beef, meatloaf seasoning, ketchup, bread crumbs, and egg. Mix until just combined; do not overmix. Shape into hot dog forms.

3. Grill for approximately 8 to 10 minutes. Serve on hot dog buns with additional ketchup, relish, and chopped onions (optional).

Banana S'Mores

makes 3 bananas **prep time** 10 minutes
cooking time 10 minutes

Even the most finicky chefs will go bananas over these S'Mores, a re-vamped campfire classic oozing with melted chocolate, marshmallows, and crumbled graham crackers.

- 3   whole large bananas, unpeeled
- ¼   cup mini chocolate morsels, *Nestlé*®
- ¼   cup mini marshmallows
- ¼   cup crushed graham crackers, *HoneyMaid*®

1. Preheat oven to 350 degrees F.

2. Place each banana on a flat surface; peel back 1½-inch wide section of the peel (do not peel completely off; just create a flap, stopping near the end of the banana). Use a spoon to scoop out lengthwise grooves in the fruit. Fill the grooves evenly with chocolate morsels. Add marshmallows and top with crushed graham crackers.

3. Replace the peeled sections on top and wrap the bananas in foil. Bake about 10 minutes.

Frozen Bananas

makes 8 banana halves **prep time** 10 minutes
freezing time 1 hour 20 minutes

Instead of Popsicles®, pop a banana in the freezer for a nutritious grab-and-eat treat. Decorate with chocolate chips, chopped nuts, or candy confetti for all-in-one fun.

- 8   wooden crafts sticks
- 4   bananas, peeled and cut in half
- 1   cup semisweet chocolate morsels, *Nestlé*®
- 1   cup butterscotch morsels, *Nestlé*®
- 1   cup chopped almonds, *Diamond*®
- 1   cup candy sprinkles

1. Insert wooden stick into each banana piece. Arrange on parchment- or foil-lined tray and freeze for 20 minutes.

2. Place chocolate and butterscotch morsels into 2 separate bowls. Microwave on medium heat for 60 seconds, stirring every 30 seconds. Remove bananas from freezer and dip first in melted chocolate and then in butterscotch. Immediately roll them in chopped nuts or sprinkles.

3. Return bananas to lined tray and place in the freezer for 1 hour.

Fish and Chips with Tartar Sauce

servings 4 **prep time** 30 minutes
cooking time 20 minutes

Fish Fry

Vegetable oil, *Wesson*®
3 **cups dry wheat breakfast cereal squares**
1 **cup all-purpose flour, *Pillsbury*®**
1 **packet (1-ounce) dry ranch salad dressing mix, *Hidden Valley*®**
1/8 **teaspoon salt**
1 **pound halibut fillets, cut into 3×1-inch strips**
2 **eggs, lightly beaten**

Chips

1 **pound (16 ounces) frozen fries, *Ore-Ida Extra Crispy Golden Crinkles*®**
Seasoning, *McCormick*® *Salt-Free All-Purpose Seasoning*®

Tartar Sauce

1/4 **cup sweet relish**
1 **cup mayonnaise, *Best Foods*® or *Hellmann's*®**
1 **teaspoon yellow mustard**
1/2 **lemon, juiced**
Salt and pepper

Fish Fry Preparation

1. Fill fryer with vegetable oil to its maximum level, or fill a deep pot no more than halfway with oil. Preheat oil in fryer or pot to 350 degrees F.

2. Fill a gallon resealable plastic bag with 3 cups wheat cereal. Using a rolling pin, lightly crush cereal into small crumbs. Set aside.

3. In a shallow bowl, combine flour, ranch dressing mix, and salt. Coat fish with seasoned flour mixture, then shake off excess flour. Dip into eggs; place in resealable bag and shake to coat in crushed cereal. Continue with remaining fillets. Carefully put 3 to 4 pieces in fryer and cook until golden brown and crisp, about 5 minutes. Repeat with remaining fillets. Serve warm with tartar sauce and seasoned chips.

Chips Preparation

4. Meanwhile, preheat oven to 450 degrees F. Arrange fries in a single layer on a sheet pan. Sprinkle liberally with seasoning. Bake for 15 minutes or until golden and crisp. Seasoning will act as a substitute for ketchup.

Tartar Sauce Preparation

5. In a small dish, strain relish and discard juices. In a separate bowl, combine strained relish with mayonnaise, mustard, and lemon juice. Stir thoroughly. Add salt and pepper to taste.

Corn Dogs

makes 12 corn dogs **prep time** 10 minutes
cooking time 12 minutes

Vegetable oil, *Wesson*®
1   **package (10-ounce) hush puppy mix,** *McCormick® Golden Dipt®*
1½ **cups milk**
2   **packets (1.42 ounces each) spaghetti sauce mix,** *Lawry's Original*
      Style Spaghetti Sauce®
½   **cup all-purpose flour,** *Pillsbury®*
12 **wooden sticks**
12 **reduced-fat beef franks,** *Hebrew National®*

1. Fill fryer with vegetable oil to its maximum level, or fill a deep pot no more than halfway with oil. Preheat oil in fryer or pot to 360 degrees F.

2. Meanwhile, in a large bowl, combine hush puppy mix, milk, and 1 of the seasoning packets. In a separate shallow dish, mix the remaining seasoning packet and flour.

3. Insert wooden sticks halfway into beef franks. Dredge each beef frank in the flour-seasoning mixture, dusting off excess flour. Dip each beef frank into the hush puppy batter. Fry 2 to 3 corn dogs at a time for about 3 minutes or until golden brown. Drain on paper towels. Serve corn dogs warm.

Spicy Fries

servings 8 **prep time** 5 minutes
cooking time 12 minutes

2   **tablespoons chili seasoning mix,** *McCormick®*
1   **teaspoon salt**
1   **bag (26-ounce) frozen fries,** *Ore-Ida Extra Crispy Golden Crinkles®*

1. Preheat oven to 450 degrees F. Combine chili seasoning mix and salt; set aside.

2. On a sheet pan, make a single layer of frozen french fries. Bake 12 minutes or until golden brown. Repeat until all the french fries are done. Season with spicy salt mixture. Serve with chili dogs.

Spiced Chicken Tenders with Dipping Sauces

servings 4 **prep time** 15 minutes
cooking time 18 minutes

My nephew Brycer loves chicken tenders. My version has a healthful twist kids adore—they're double dipped in buttermilk to make them extra tender, then again in corn bran cereal for a light, flaky crust. Dunked in a sweet and tangy marinara sauce, they bring smiles by the miles.

Tenders
Vegetable oil, *Wesson*®
½   **cup all-purpose flour, *Pillsbury*®**
½   **packet (½ of a 1.25-ounce packet) Southwest marinade mix,**
    ***McCormick*® *Grill Mates*®**
    Ground black pepper
3   **cups corn bran cereal**
1   **egg, lightly beaten**
½   **cup buttermilk**
1   **pound chicken breast tenders**

Dipping Sauces
1   **cup ketchup**
1½ **cups honey, *Sue Bee*®**
    Dash Worcestershire sauce, *Lea & Perrins*®
1   **cup yellow mustard, *French's*®**

Tenders Preparation
1. Fill a fryer with oil to its maximum level, or fill a deep pot no more than halfway with oil. Preheat oil in fryer or pot to 375 degrees F.

2. In a large resealable bag, combine flour, marinade mix, and pepper. Set aside. In another bag, add corn bran. Using a rolling pin, gently crush cereal to coarse ground crumbs. Set aside. In a shallow bowl, combine egg and buttermilk.

3. Soak chicken strips in buttermilk mixture. Toss a few strips at a time in seasoned flour mixture. Shake off excess flour and dip into buttermilk mixture again. Toss chicken in cereal crumbs to coat. Repeat with remaining chicken strips.

4. Fry chicken strips in batches until golden brown and cooked through, about 6 to 7 minutes per batch. Drain on paper towels. Serve warm with dipping sauces.

Dipping Sauces Preparation
5. For the ketchup dipping sauce, in a small bowl, combine ketchup, ½ cup of the honey, and the Worcestershire sauce.

6. For the mustard dipping sauce, in a small bowl, combine the remaining 1 cup honey and the mustard.

Churros

makes 16 churros **prep time** 10 minutes
cooking time 4 minutes

Vegetable Oil, *Wesson*®
6   **tablespoons granulated sugar,** *C&H*®
1   **tablespoon ground cinnamon,** *McCormick*®
1   **egg**
3   **tablespoons butter, melted and cooled slightly**
¹⁄₂ **cup milk**
2¹⁄₄ **cups all-purpose baking mix,** *Bisquick*®

1. Pour oil into a 10-inch heavy skillet to a depth of 1 inch. Preheat to 350 degrees F. In a small bowl, combine 4 tablespoons of the sugar and the cinnamon.

2. In a large bowl, beat egg with butter. Stir in milk. Gradually stir in baking mix and the remaining 2 tablespoons sugar. Spoon mixture into a piping bag fitted with a star tip.

3. Pipe dough in lines, a few at a time, into the skillet of hot oil. Fry about 30 seconds on each side or just until a deep golden color. Drain on paper towels. While still hot, sprinkle with cinnamon-sugar mixture.

Tip: Use a new Play-Doh® Fun Factory to get fun shapes for your Churros. Cut dough in 3- to 4-inch pieces and fry as directed above. Your kids will love it!

Funnel Cakes

makes 4 cakes **prep time** 10 minutes
cooking time 20 minutes

Vegetable oil, *Wesson*®
3   **cups all-purpose baking mix,** *Bisquick*®
2   **eggs, lightly beaten**
$^1/_2$ **cup milk**
1   **cup liquid French vanilla coffee creamer,** *International Delight*®
          (or substitute other creamer flavors)
     Powdered sugar, *C&H*®

1. Fill fryer with vegetable oil to its maximum level, or fill a deep pot no more than halfway with oil. Preheat oil in fryer or pot to 375 degrees F.

2. In a large mixing bowl, combine baking mix, eggs, milk, and coffee creamer. Beat with electric mixer until combined, about 3 minutes.

3. Spoon batter into a self sealing plastic bag. Snip the corner from the bag and pipe batter over oil, moving in a spiral motion.

4. Fry funnel cake for 2 to 3 minutes on each side or until golden brown on both sides. Drain on paper towels and dust with powdered sugar.

Cupcake Layer Cake

makes 1 cake (12 servings) and 24 cupcakes
prep time 25 minutes **cooking time** see package directions on cake mix **cooling time** 1 hour

Cupcakes or cake? Served together, they're twice as nice. This playful centerpiece dessert has a polka dot cake on the bottom, topped with a tower of rainbow-colored cupcakes—all flavored with creamy marshmallow. For a change, substitute fruit juice in place of water for a child's party and Champagne in place of water for an adult occasion.

Layer Cake
1   box (18.25-ounce) moist butter cake mix, *Betty Crocker SuperMoist*®
1½ teaspoons marshmallow flavoring

Cupcakes
1   box (18.25-ounce) moist butter cake mix, *Betty Crocker SuperMoist*®

Decoration
4   containers (16 ounces each) white buttercream frosting, *Betty Crocker Whipped*®
6   teaspoons marshmallow flavoring
     Food coloring (such as blue, red, green, and yellow), *McCormick*®
     Plastic sandwich bags

Layer Cake Preparation
1. Prepare and bake 1 box of cake mix according to package directions, adding marshmallow flavoring, to make one 2-layer round cake (8- or 9-inch).

Cupcake Preparation
2. For cupcakes, prepare and bake remaining box of cake mix according to package directions to make 24 cupcakes.

Cake Assembly and Decoration
3. To assemble, sandwich the 2 cake layers together with ½ cup buttercream. If necessary, flatten top layer by evenly cutting off the top horizontally. Cover the sides and top of cake with remaining frosting from first container. If necessary, use another container of frosting. Smooth frosting. Place in refrigerator and let chill for 1 hour.

4. Divide remaining 2 containers of frosting into 4 bowls. Add 1½ teaspoons marshmallow flavoring to each bowl. Add a different color of food coloring to each bowl of frosting.

5. Fill 4 small sandwich bags with about ½ cup of each color frosting. Snip a small hole in one corner of each bag and pipe varying sizes of dots onto the layer cake.

6. Frost cupcakes with remaining colored buttercream frosting. Arrange and stack 11 frosted cupcakes in a 3-level pyramid on top of the cake: 7 cupcakes on the bottom layer, 3 on the middle layer, and 1 cupcake on top.

Kids' Cranberry Citrus Punch

makes about 2 quarts
prep time 5 minutes

1   (12-ounce) can frozen cranberry concentrate
3½ cups fresh orange juice, *Minute Maid*®
1   liter lemon-lime soda

1. Combine cranberry concentrate, orange juice, and lemon-lime soda in a pitcher. Divide into smaller pitchers for easy serving. Serve in glasses over ice.

Lemon Icee

servings 6
prep time 5 minutes

1   can (12-ounce) frozen lemonade mix concentrate
2   tablespoons packaged lemon gelatin mix, *Jell-O*®
1   tablespoon granulated sugar, *C&H*®
     Ice

1. In a blender, pulse lemonade, gelatin, and sugar. Add ice to almost fill blender and continue to pulse until ice is crushed. Pour into glasses and serve.

A Tip from Brycer: When making lemonade from frozen concentrate, Brycer uses soda water instead of plain water to give it old-fashioned fizz and fun.

Index

Index (cont.)